Liberalism and Conservatism

Liberalism and Conservatism

Edited by
Greg Melleuish

Connor Court Publishing
Ballarat

Published by Connor Court Publishing Pty Ltd

Copyright © Greg Melleuish (as a collection), 2015

ALL RIGHTS RESERVED. This book contains material protected under International and Federal Copyright Laws and Treaties. Any unauthorised reprint or use of this material is prohibited. No part of this book may be reproduced or transmitted in any form or by any means, electronic or mechanical, including photocopying, recording, or by any information storage and retrieval system without express written permission from the publisher.

PO Box 224W
Ballarat VIC 3350
sales@connorcourt.com
www.connorcourt.com

ISBN: 978-1-925138-59-7

Cover design by Maria Giordano

Photo from istockphoto

Printed in Australia

Contents

Acknowledgements

Introduction: Liberalism and Conservatism
-- Greg Melleuish   1

1. George Reid's Anti-Socialist Campaign in the Evolution of Australian Liberalism
-- Zachary Gorman   17

2. Liberalism, Conservatism and the Growth of Government in Australia
-- David Kemp   39

3. The Progressive Conservatism of Alexander Downer: The Meta-Narrative of Resistance, Family Heritage and Edmund Burke
-- Paul Brown   97

4. Conservatism in Australia
-- Greg Melleuish   121

5. Australian Conservatives and the Politics of Science
-- Wayne Errington   141

6. What I wasn't taught at High School
-- Chris Rath   157

Acknowledgements

This book has its origins in a Workshop held at the University of Wollongong on Australian conservatism in November 2012. It was funded by a Near Miss grant awarded to me by the University of Wollongong. In particular I should like to thank those people who helped to organise that day, Kerry Duff and Leonie Clements.

I should also like to thank Steve Chavura who has done the formatting of the book and made it presentable to be sent to the publisher. Steve has been doing research on my Discovery project DP DP140100246 of which my contributions to this book form part.

Finally, I should like to thank Anthony Cappello for the support that he has given to my work over the years.

Greg Melleuish

Introduction

Liberalism and Conservatism

Greg Melleuish

How do liberalism and conservatism fit into our understanding of Australian history and politics?

There has been a tendency to underplay them and to pretend that Australian political culture is somehow naturally radical or even social democratic as befits a 'new' settler society.[1] The story runs from Chartism to the formation of the Labor Party to the Social laboratory to reconstruction to the Whitlam government, although after 1975 the narrative runs out of steam. Any attempt to construct a liberal equivalent of this narrative soon runs into the problem that the Labor/radical narrative casts non-Labor in the role of being a "party of resistance" seeking only to wind back those "progressive" things which Labor has done.[2]

At another level, however, liberalism has been ubiquitous in Australia. This is the consequence of Australia being essentially a 'contract' as opposed to a 'status' society in which its members are understood as individuals and not as 'patrons' and 'clients', as members of an extended lineage.[3] There were attempts to import elements of 'status' from Britain, including an attempt to establishment a colonial landed aristocracy, but these came to nothing. The notion that landowners might stand at the head of their subordinate 'tenants' was tried but never amounted to much in Australia. The fact that female suffrage was created so early in Australia is an indication of the weakness of patriarchal status social structures in Australia. One of the few places where traditional patron-

---

1 Richard H. Rosencrance, 'The Radical Culture of Australia,' in Louis Hartz, *The Founding of New Societies*, New York: Harcourt, Brace & World, 1964, pp.275-318.
2 W. K. Hancock, *Australia*, London: Benn, 1930, Chapters X & XI.
3 On 'status' and 'contract' see Henry Sumner Maine, *Ancient Law*, 4th Ed. London: John Murray, 1870, p.170.

client relationships appear to have persisted in Australia has been in its universities.

One consequence of Australia being a contract society, and hence liberal, has been the fact that conservatism in Australia has largely been of the liberal variety, or at least operates within a framework created by liberalism, which is to say that it has often consisted of the defence of particular liberal values. This is not say that Australia is a specifically Benthamite society in which utilitarianism has reigned supreme.[4] Australian liberalism may contain utilitarian components but it is firmly rooted in a variety of traditions including constitutional traditionalism and English common law.

Why then, if liberalism has been ubiquitous in Australia, has there been a tendency to deny its importance?

- The word 'liberal' is attached to one of the two major political parties and the term 'liberal' is therefore 'tainted' by the reality of practical politics. It could be construed that in saying that Australia owes a considerable debt to 'liberalism' is the same as saying that it owes a lot to the Liberal Party.
- If the Liberal Party is described in some circles as the 'party of resistance' then this also indicates that liberalism is not a progressive element of Australian political culture.
- There appears to be something unheroic about the triumph of English liberalism in Australia, something pedestrian and bourgeois. This attitude is found most strikingly in Manning Clark's History of Australia where Clark looks for tragic heroes to play off against what he sees as the plodding bourgeois values of Australia's British inheritance. This fits in with a more general attitude to what is perceived as the 'boring' quality of the history of Australia. This is the intellectual's disdain for the 'provincial' society in which he or she was raised. Bourgeois academics who have benefitted through living in a liberal society bemoan that they do not live in a more dangerous and unpleasant place, primarily because they do not appreciate how awful such a place would be.

A number of important points can be made regarding the nature of Australian politics and political culture:
- Australian society has always been a society of individuals and their

---

[4] Hugh Collins, 'Political Ideology in Australia: The Distinctiveness of a Benthamite Society', *Daedalus*, Vol. 114, No 1, Winter 1985: pp.147-169.

families. Individualism has always been central to the way in which Australians have understood themselves. Two examples of this individualism can be seen in the fact that the Australian colonies were the first to make use of the secret ballot and amongst the first to grant the franchise to women. The secret ballot assumes that an elector is an individual and must be left free to consult his (and later her) conscience when exercising that franchise. Granting the vote to women was recognition that women were more than just appendages to their husbands and fathers; they were individuals capable of choosing freely who would represent them.

- The individualism of Australian politics was a consequence, at least in part, of what can be termed the particular 'cultural patterning' which the Australian colonies had inherited from Britain.[5] As Alan MacFarlane has demonstrated this individualism is deeply rooted in English culture.[6] It manifested itself in Australian politics in a number of ways, including utilitarianism and the appeal to conscience. In the early days of responsible government it found expression in the faction system of politics which revolved around what were essentially charismatic leaders who attracted followers on the basis of their personalities and capacities.[7] Independence was valued as desirable quality for an individual to possess, just as it is described as a most desirable characteristic in J. S. Mill's *On Liberty*, a work which had great influence in Australia.
- Even in the more collectivist twentieth century it is clear that individualism remained central for many Australians. Look at W. K. Hancock's *Australia* and R. G. Menzies' *The Forgotten People*. As I have argued elsewhere, there is also good evidence to support the idea that distributivism (or distributism) has a long history in Australia, and not just in Catholic circles.[8] Distributivism is not socialist as it does not support the collective ownership of property. Instead it seeks to spread property ownership as widely as possible as a means of strengthening the individual.

---

5 On cultural patterning see Marshall G. S. Hodgson, *Rethinking World History: Essays on Europe, Islam and World History*, Edmund Burke III (ed.), Cambridge: Cambridge University Press, 1993, Chapter 8.
6 Alan Macfarlane, *The Origins of English Individualism*, Oxford: Blackwell, 1968.
7 P. Loveday and A. W. Martin, *Parliament, factions and parties: the first thirty years of responsible government in New South Wales 1856–1889*, Melbourne: Melbourne University Press, 1966.
8 Greg Melleuish, 'Distributivism: The Australian Political Ideal?', *Journal of Australian Studies*, 1999, 62: pp.20-9.

- More recent debates regarding welfare and the growth of the state are not so much about individualism versus collectivism as the correct means of ensuring that individuals possess a measure of independence and dignity.

It is a reality that liberals of all descriptions support the idea of a strong state even if they argue about the extent of state interference in the lives of individuals. They are not anarchists and most certainly are perfectly aware of the many problems which arise when a state lacks power and authority. Hobbes was wrong on this matter; Mark Weiner in his recent book *The Rule of the Clan* points out that the alternative to the state is a society composed of clans in which the individual is subsumed into the larger group.[9] The individual, in the liberal sense, can only come into existence when the clan ceases to exert influence over its members. The state replaces the clan as the upholder of public order. Hence as there have never been clans in Australia, the state has always exercised primacy.

However, as Wiener points out, some clan societies can be quite democratic, citing the case of medieval Iceland. The growth of the modern state most certainly possesses despotic tendencies as it accumulates more and more power into its hands. One of the most important features of a modern liberal democracy is the growth of the state and its ever-expanding capacity to control its members.

While it is clear that we cannot do without a strong state (who wants to have to carry a gun every time they leave home?) the most important issue of the contemporary political world revolves around how extensive the powers of the state should be. Progressive liberals, who are also known as social liberals, are happy to extend the powers of the state in the name of helping and what they see as 'empowering' people. More traditional liberals see such extension of state power as simply empowering the state.

Liberal conservatism in Australia takes the form of restraining the power of the state and providing the opportunity for individuals to solve their own problems rather than relying on the government. The cultural roots of this individualism have never really been explored but there is evidence that it comes out of a distinctive sense of self found in large parts of the British Isles. It resonates with the various forms of British Protestantism. It also emerges out of the idea of the

---

[9] Mark Weiner, *The Rule of the Clan*, New York: Farrar, Straus & Giroux, 2013.

independent yeoman and the republican idea that an individual who can support himself on his own property does not need to rely on anyone. This desire for independence inspired movements seeking free selection in nineteenth century Australia; individuals sought above all else to be responsible for their actions and not to be subservient to someone of supposedly higher social standing. Such independent individuals see the world as being composed of people like themselves who consult their conscience as the basis for their behaviour.

The liberal desire that one should be able to act as a free self-determining individual is the product of a long and complex social, cultural and political evolution. Modern individuals are not 'natural' entities; individuals do not exist in traditional societies in which family groups rule the roost. Larry Siedentop has recently demonstrated how the individual emerged in the West.[10] It was a long and involved process.

The point is that when British settlers came to Australia they brought with them ideas about liberty and individualism which were the product of a long cultural evolution. There were very few settlers who could be described as a conservative in the metropolitan sense; they were generally liberals but liberals who owed their liberalism to traditional understandings of politics, not abstract thinkers who started from first principles. They were liberals who wished to conserve what they saw as the best traditions of the society from which they had come.

One way of considering this matter is to say that the Australian colonists desired to be progressive and liberal in a British fashion because to do so was to guarantee stability and order. Liberalism could be portrayed as a conservative doctrine which ensured that even in a new strange land the traditions of the home society would be maintained and even enhanced. Ideals of progress were important because they confirmed the *telos* which governed the process of colonisation and ensured that the project on which they were engaged would be fulfilled. Stadial theories of progress combined with a faith in a world governed by laws, such as economic laws which would create a peaceful harmonious world in which free trade ruled, and a belief in beneficent providence ensured that the world was not a plaything of contingency and chance. It was a place where one could be assured that if they behaved in in accordance with the natural order everything would be alright.[11] Liberalism seemed

---

10 Larry Siedentop, *Inventing the Individual: The Origins of Western Liberalism*, London: Allen & Lane, 2014.
11 Greg Melleuish, 'Beneficent Providence and the Quest for Harmony: The Cultural Setting

to guarantee ordered change that would lead to a secure future. A free people would be enabled to make the correct decisions, decisions based on natural or God's laws. That meant staying on the straight and narrow path which led from past to future. It did not mean being daring, taking risks or engaging in innovation. Nineteenth century Australian liberals were at heart quite conservative.

I would like to illustrate the problem of understanding the conservatism of an inherently liberal society by a small, but not irrelevant example. In the second half of the 1850s the three major colonies were granted responsible government. Within a short time they had all moved to institute what were, at the time, radical democratic measures, namely universal manhood suffrage and the secret ballot. By 1860 in New South Wales the 'conservative' element of politics had been routed, some conservatives had even left the colony, and nearly every political figure called himself a liberal. There was, at the public level, very little support for traditional conservatism. How could there be? There was no established church, no aristocracy.

J. S. Mill's *On Liberty* reached the colonies in the first half of 1859. It was the topic for an editorial in the *Sydney Morning Herald* and the Melbourne *Argus* in May 1859 and an article in the Sydney *Empire* a year later. The reception of what was perhaps the most famous liberal tract of its age by these newspapers tells us something about what both liberalism and conservatism meant at this crucial point in the development of Australian politics. It is clear that all three newspapers are advocates of the ideal of liberty but it is their discussion of what they understand by liberty and its relationship to other values that we can discern an indication of what liberalism would eventually come to mean in Australia.

How then did these three newspapers, located in advanced democratic societies, respond to the work of the greatest liberal of the day?

The *Argus* contended that *On Liberty* demonstrated the "growing power of society over the individual, whether the force exerted take the shape of opinion or of legislation, and the arbitrary and despotic tendencies of that power."[12] It claimed that there was a tyranny abroad which threatened modern liberal society and argued that Mill's harm principle meets this difficulty thereby ensuring that individuals are not

---

for Colonial Science in Sydney 1850–1890', *Journal and Proceedings, Royal Society of New South Wales*, 118, 1985: pp.167-80.
12 *Argus*, 18 May 1859, p.4.

subject to coercion but able to exercise their powers freely.

It saw the harm principle in these terms:

> By the principle above laid down, perfect liberty of conscience, of thought, feeling and speech, of tastes and pursuits, of framing the plan of his own life in accordance with the bent of his own genius, of combination with others for purposes not harmful to society, and of promulgating opinions and sentiments (subject to obvious limitations) is claimed for the individual; and it is assumed that no society in which this liberty is not respected can be free, no matter what its form of government; and that mankind will be necessarily gainers by sanctioning this absolute freedom, instead of compelling each to conform to the will and practice of the rest.

Mr. Mill, it continued, advocates "the erection of such a strong barrier of moral conviction as shall resist the further progress of this evil, and pointing out the degeneracy of civilisation as the inevitable consequence of the unlimited authority which society bids fair to establish over the individual."

Individual liberty is the motor of progress, and the Australian colonies are part of this progress of civilisation. Once the road of freedom and progress has been taken there can be no backsliding, because that way lies the threat of "degeneracy" and decay. One can see why progress would be built into the DNA of Australian liberalism, as it carries the torch of civilisation to the farthest corners of the earth. That progress is threatened by "unlimited authority", be it that of the state or of society, which retards the proper course of human history. What is involved here is not a licence to do as one pleases. Rather it is a recognition of what might be termed the 'British way'; Britain has prospered and expanded because it has allowed the individual to flourish. That is the secret of its success.

The editorials in the two Sydney papers are more intellectually complex and reflect the fact that Sydney already had seventy years history behind it. The *Empire* was an unabashedly liberal paper; the *Herald* can be described as liberal conservative in orientation. It waged war against what it saw as the inadequacies of democracy, this included condemnations of the brutal attacks on Chinese miners which occurred on the Lambing Flats goldfields in 1861.

The *Empire* begins with a paean to liberty, which is what one might expect given that the *Empire* was a 'liberal' liberal newspaper which expressed the 'advanced' views of the colony of New South Wales.

> LIBERTY! The subject will never grow old, the name will never cease to arouse the warmest, deepest feelings of man's heart. Momentary disgust at maudlin eulogies dedicated to this noble word, passing indignation at the crimes committed in the name of liberty, may occasionally throw a cloud over the glorious motto; but still will "Liberty" be among the mightiest banner cries which nerve the brave and true to deeds of excellence.[13]

What is curious about the above quote is what appears to be the somewhat ambiguous attitude to liberty with "disgust" at the "maudlin eulogies" made to it, and "indignation" at the "crimes committed" in its name. It is also interesting that liberty is justified not in economic terms, as one might expect in a colony dedicated to "getting and spending", but because it provides a spur for the "brave and true" to enact "deeds of excellence". Liberty is understood in terms which might be termed aristocratic; liberty is certainly not described as something which allows an individual to maximise his or her utility. The "brave and the true" are not ways in which merchants are generally described.

The article then moves to a discussion of the harm principle. Individuals, it claims, are in charge of their own happiness; society has no right to choose it for them. Society does not possess the right to bend the will of the individual to what it believes secures happiness but there are limits to what any individual can do in relation to causing harm and it is interesting that the author sees those limits in terms of language. Language "which grossly offends against public decency or tends directly to downright immorality" cannot be allowed but must be supressed by the law. It is difficult to know exactly what sort of language is meant but what this argument indicates is the idea of an established moral order which cannot be transgressed. Liberty means freedom of action within a specified moral framework. Society does prescribe what individuals can do to secure their happiness in the sense that happiness is constrained by moral order, and there are penalties for those who seek their happiness outside of this order, or at least publicly indicate that they have moved outside of this order. This is, in many ways, quite a conservative position because it places limits on liberty, and expects that individuals will act within those limits. This would indicate that the real problem as seen by some from the Australian colonies was not so much the suppression of individualism but the need to maintain moral order and a measure of respectability.

---

13 'John Stuart Mill on Liberty', *Empire*, 26 March 1860, p.2.

Such an outlook can be seen in the response of the author to Mill's complaints regarding the "tyranny of the majority". Our author sets out to defend the majority from the claims of any minority as follows:

> Freedom of criticism for the masses must accompany freedom of utterance for individuals; and the one operates a healthful check against the abuses of the other.

Individuals have the right to liberty but that right has limits; the majority also has the right to protect itself against what it sees as harmful effects which might arise from the use of that liberty by particular individuals. For this author the issue is not the exercise of liberty as an end in itself but the need for truth to manifest itself, even if there are problems in discerning exactly what that truth is. The objective of the exercise of liberty is the emergence of truth from error.

> The only way in which the truth, and all the benefits resulting from a clear knowledge of it, can be secured to the community, is by the exercise of the fullest freedom on both sides in advocating and in criticising the disputed truth.

This leads to a rather curious discussion regarding individualism in which the author appears to argue that individualism is a quality peculiar to the contemporary period which is placed between two ages of unity. The past was characterised by "compulsory and hollow unities." The future will see "a unity arising out of free unprejudiced research and universal knowledge of truth." The current age is one which "exhibits the marvellous vagaries of individualism" because it is an age of transition; human beings have escaped "mere prescription" but have not arrived at an age of science marked by "patient, honest and laborious investigation." Once individuals have the opportunity to look at matters in a thoughtful, relaxed and patient fashion presumably liberty will become redundant because there will be acknowledged truth.

The article is saying that liberty is desirable, not as good in itself, but because it provides a mechanism through which a community can aspire to truth. It provides the route to a future social order which will be marked by truth; it may indicate a current lack of social cohesion but eventually it is the only means through which social harmony will ultimately be achieved. Truth, and the organisation of the social order according to truth, is the real goal. Liberty is but a means to an end.

Given the nature of this argument it is worth asking: who wrote this article? If it were not for the rather plain and unadorned prose I would suggest John Woolley, the Principal of the University of Sydney. Woolley certainly wrote for the *Empire*, and the emphasis on truth, as opposed to liberty, would fit in with Woolley's Platonism.

The *Sydney Morning Herald* leader, which can be presumed to have been written by the editor John West, took a different approach. It argued that Mill had exaggerated the "evils" of what it termed "conventionalism" and to have ignored "the advantages that may grow out of it."[14] The *SMH* emphasised the need for social unity and the necessity for "some sacrifice of individualism"; custom was an essential part of being human. "*Ubi homines stint, mores sunt*," the leader continued. Society must be "an organic whole", not "a congeries of particles." This leads to a discussion of the reasons why individuals need to prune and curb "the rebellious luxuriance of self-will," through such means as good manners, public morality and patriotism, and the "individual sacrifice for the public weal." "The advancement alike of the individual as of the species," it claimed, "is promoted as much by self-denial as by self-expression."

Why was self-denial and creating an organic whole so important for West? Did it come out of a fear that the progressive, democratic society of colonial Australia might yet descend into a "congeries of particles"? West engaged in a long-term criticism of the workings of democracy in NSW. His criticism was founded on the unsuitability of many of the people who sought and won public office. In an article appearing in the *Herald* at much the same time as the discussion of Mill can be found the following description of such a candidate for public office:

> Unable to speak five consecutive English words correctly, but having borrowed all his imagery from the lowest walks of life, his addresses are in the highest degree terse and taking. He dances with the girls; "shouts" with the men; promises a millennium of similar joys: and has, we are told, really a prospect of honouring the floor of our future Assembly with his presence.
>
> But what advantage can a country gain from having its legislation committed to men whose special knowledge and peculiar experience will be of no value to their own class, and who are totally incapable of comprehending the general interests of the country, or of seeing beyond the circle of a quart pot?[15]

Having defended conventionalism against what he saw as the excesses of individualism West then turned his attention to the other side of the

---

14 *Sydney Morning Herald*, 31 May 1859, p.4.
15 *Sydney Morning Herald*, 18 April 1859, p.4.

argument conceding that "there is plenty of room for protest against the tyranny of modern organisations, whether social, political, educational, or religious." The problem with modern society, he argued, was that the group has come to dominate the individual

> There is no room for eccentricity. It is so in politics. A man must belong to a party or he is nowhere. If he agrees a little with both sides, and cannot attach himself heartily to either-still more, if he differs fundamentally from both, he is left behind as a useless crotchetty fellow.

West recognises that arguments regarding the tyranny of the majority have a strong foundation in reality, after all he is a member of a democratic community not an outside observer of one. "For", he continues, "government by majorities leads to the counting of men as so much force available on one side or the other, and takes no note of any other kind of worth." He completes his analysis with the following:

> Yet, as CARLYLE is fond of telling the world, all the great systems and creeds that have ever found a footing had their origin in "minorities of one." And in this respect, history will doubtless continue to repeat itself. The struggle between individualism and conventionalism will endure till the world is perfect-till society is so tolerant as to offer no restraint to the fullest expression of personality, and personality develops itself so rightly as to offer no offence to society. And when will that be?

When indeed?

There is much disagreement in these various responses to *On Liberty*. What one writer sees as an age of individualism another sees as the age of regimentation. It demonstrates that within that thing which we can call 'colonial liberalism' there are a range of views and emphases. The exercise of liberty by free individuals does not lead to agreement or to something which can be labelled 'truth.' Moreover these articles indicate that liberalism can be more, or less, 'liberal', more, or less, 'conservative', according to the individual concerned.

But what is striking is that both of the Sydney writers, in defending the virtues of liberty and its benefits seem unwilling to defend Mill's radical individualism and his defence of creative minorities as the motor of progress in society. *The Empire*, seen as a liberal newspaper in a liberal age takes the side of the 'tyrannical' majority and its need to defend itself. There must be freedom of expression on both sides. Mill, it can be argued, was primarily concerned with liberty for the progressive elements of society struggling against conventionalism.

The *Sydney Morning Herald* equally remained unconvinced that virtue lay solely on the side of the individual struggling against social convention. Customs, conventions and good manners are all essential for the maintenance of social order. One must sacrifice a degree of individualism for the social good.

Both writers look to a future where individualism might be reconciled with social order, where individual will and social convention are in harmony. But neither, despite being defenders of liberty, is willing to let the individual off the leash. They do not want to turn the world over to the Millian creative elite. Perhaps this is a piece of evidence which indicates that Australian political culture instinctively owes more to Burke than to Mill. The understanding of liberty in both of these leaders can be described as having a conservative orientation. Liberty is understood as a good, but as a good to be exercised within a corporate framework so that there is a balance between the individual and the wider society. What both writers seem to desire is a social order in which there is a harmony between individual will and social conformity.

I think that this reflects the values of a settler society which simultaneously sees itself as progressive and liberal *and* preserving the institutions and political culture of the metropolitan as part of their inheritance. John Hirst has been critical of the failure of this colonial society to become more radically democratic, for its one time radical politicians to happily accept knighthoods and to accept the empire in all its glory.[16] It is also the case that many of these radicals would become critics of the failings of the democracy which they had helped to create. It had created a liberal and democratic political order but one which was fundamentally conservative in its orientation.

Certainly a good case can be made that subsequently there has been no extended discourse of liberty in Australia which celebrates the word as an ideal in itself. In the nineteenth century liberty was understood in a concrete sense, as part of the inheritance the colonists had brought with them from Britain. It was central to their being in the world, of their way in which they conducted politics. All of it made sense while Australians looked to Britain for inspiration to fulfil their political ideals. Liberty was not important as an abstract ideal but as a form of practice.

At a later stage in Australia, when the need arose to adopt a more theoretical approach to the world, there was a tendency to confuse liberty

---

16 John Hirst, *The Strange Birth of Colonial Democracy*, Sydney: Allen & Unwin, 1988.

with efficiency. In many ways this goes back to the positions expressed above; the goal has never been liberty as such. Liberty is a means of creating an order in which individual and society are in harmony. Efficiency has a similar goal. The ideal is a stable, corporate order which will not disintegrate into a "congeries of particles" and which provide protection against a potentially threatening world.

The complexity of the relationship between liberalism and conservatism is reflected in this collection of what are truly ground breaking essays on Australian liberalism and conservatism. They provide a new set of perspectives on the liberal and conservative traditions of thought in Australia. Liberalism, in particular, is revealed as both a set of political principles and as a set of ideas which have changed and evolved over the years as circumstances have changed.

Zachary Gorman's chapter describes how liberalism in Australia was crystallised by George Reid's 1906 anti-socialism campaign. The rise of the Australian Labor Party and its adoption of a political program increasingly framed by socialist ideas meant that liberalism no longer so completely ruled the roost in Australia as it had since the granting of responsible government in the 1850s. Faced by this challenge liberals could no longer afford to engage in disputes and fights amongst themselves, such has occurred for over twenty years regarding the fiscal issue. Liberals needed to determine for what they stood, and Reid's campaign set out to do this.

Gorman points out that the campaign was both a failure and a success. It was a failure in that it did not deliver government to the Anti-Socialists in the 1906 election, a success in that the Anti-Socialists received the most votes of any party at the election. Gorman identifies Deakin as the villain of the peace, so tied to protection that he was unwilling to grasp the bigger picture.

Nevertheless it was anti-Socialism, or more positively liberal individualism, which became the foundation of the Liberal Party created by fusion in 1909, a testament to the hard work which Reid had put in three years earlier. Deakin led the new party, but it was the former free trader Joseph Cook who led it to its first election victory.

It is the period between World War I and the re—creation of the Liberal Party by Sir Robert Menzies which is the most troubling and difficult to explain for Australian liberals. This was period in which the non-Labor side of politics moved from liberalism to nationalism to a vague pragmatism, and was led for long periods of time by former

Labor men. As Michael Roe has argued, something strange happened to Australian culture after World War I. The pre-World War I world was very different from our own. Above all it owed its vision of the world to a liberalism which was not statist in outlook. Hence, as David Kemp argues, the original Labor Party was not statist; it was essentially another expression of nineteenth century voluntarism seeking to get the best possible deal for its members. It was only in the early years of the twentieth century that the state became a fetish of Australian politics, a development exacerbated by the war years.

It was in these years that Australian liberalism lost its way, perhaps overwhelmed by events. What David Kemp's chapter demonstrates is the key role of Sir Robert Menzies in leading the non-Labor forces back to their liberal roots, from his activism in the 1920s through to the re-birth of the Liberal Party and his time as Prime Minister. He establishes a powerful case for seeing liberalism as central to Menzies' career. Kemp also demonstrates the crucial role which the Menzies government played in restraining state power and preventing its growth. The rot only really set in in 1972.

Paul Brown provides yet another dimension to the study of liberalism and conservatism in Australia with his essay on Alexander Downer and the Downer family. Brown illustrates the value of seeing political traditions through the prism of their embodiment in particular families. The Downer family's 'progressive conservatism', founded, as Brown argues, on the ideas of Edmund Burke and John Stuart Mill, has played a role in Australian public life for one hundred and fifty years. And it has been a positive role. The activities of the Downers illustrate the nonsense of the old hoary view of the Liberal Party as a party of resistance. They have been the agents of sound liberal change while also seeking to conserve what is best in the political values which Australia inherited from Britain and which form the basis of its political culture.

Wayne Errington examines the rather vexed issue of the relationship between conservatism and science in contemporary Australia, in particular climate change. He argues cogently that positions taken for, and against, climate change have as much to do with political and social attitudes as with the science lying behind it. Liberals tend to emphasise risk taking while Labor can be seen as both collectivist and risk averse. Hence liberals and conservatives are far less likely to accept arguments based on the 'precautionary principle', the underlying principle of most climate change activism. It will be interesting to see how these value differences would play out if, as some scientists are predicting, the earth is about to enter a period of short term cooling.

Finally Chris Rath explores the disaster which is Australia's national school curriculum. He points out that it only reflects the sorts of things which are already being taught in schools. Christianity, capitalism, the nation state and the law are all forces which have helped to create the world we live in and they are either avoided or denigrated. They are also forces which have moulded, or have acted in tandem with, liberalism in Australia. To fail to appreciate them is like having no knowledge of one's family and from where they came.

The essays in this volume are fresh and alive. They indicate the massive contribution made by liberalism and conservatism in Australia as intellectual forces which have moulded Australian culture. Hopefully they will set the stage for more scholarly work on this topic thereby leading to a re-evaluation of Australian history and political life, one which recognises the ways in which both liberalism and conservatism have contributed to make Australia the country which it is today.

1

George Reid's Anti-Socialist Campaign in the Evolution of Australian Liberalism

Zachary Gorman

Since the fall of the 'Australian settlement' a large amount of political history has been written that focuses on the discontinuity between the interventionist and Keynesian Liberal Party of the Menzies era and the more neo-liberal modern Liberal Party.[17] While this change in the economic policy of the party is an important historical trend, the historiographical emphasis on the difference between the Menzies and modern Liberal Parties has meant that the rhetorical and ideological continuity between the two has been ignored. Robert Menzies' fight against the nationalisation of banks and modern Liberal attacks on the mining and carbon taxes both stem from an anti-socialist ideology that at the federal level dates back to George Reid. Although the terms of reference have changed from a moralistic denunciation of a tyrannical communist state to an economic attack on excessive government spending, the Liberal Party of Australia has maintained an anti-socialist discourse and ideology that the Commonwealth Liberal Party inherited from Reid's anti-socialist campaign. Many of the most important and eternal of the debates within the Liberal Party are not fights between 'liberals' and 'conservatives' but arguments over the extent of government intervention that can be tolerated within a vaguely anti-

---

17 E.g. Norman Abjorensen, 'Three Perspectives on John Howard: The Reid Legacy, NSW Exceptionalism and the Fulfilment of Liberal Prophecy', paper delivered at the John Howard Decade Conference, Canberra, March 2006; Judith Brett, *Australian Liberals and the Moral Middle Class*, Melbourne: Cambridge University Press, 2003.

socialist framework. Recent moves away from the small government liberalism of Work Choices and towards interventionist policies like paid parental leave show that these internal debates are ongoing.

In order to understand the anti-socialism of the Liberal Party, one must analyse its origins in the anti-socialist campaign that culminated in the 1906 election. The anti-socialism Reid articulated during his campaign evolved not from reactionary fears of socialistic equality but from a liberal rejection of trade union privileges and a large and controlling state.[18] This anti-socialist ideology had been developed in Australia by liberal intellectuals such as Bruce Smith and brought into political prominence in New South Wales through the efforts of Joseph Carruthers.[19] Reid took this anti-socialist liberal ideology and popularised it through his anti-socialist campaign. Though he did not win the 1906 election his efforts meant that when the fiscal issue of protectionism versus free-trade was finally settled the Liberal side of Australian politics adopted anti-socialism as its ideological cause. It is important to note that even at the beginning there were internal debates about the proper limits of state intervention within the anti-socialist movement. Reid's liberal anti-socialist ideology was flexible enough to accommodate these differing views, thus it enabled the 'broad church' of Australian liberalism to come together.

Any analysis of the anti-socialist campaign must begin with a look at George Reid's intellectual background. Reid's anti-socialist ideology grew out of the colonial liberalism of nineteenth century Australia. In the 1840's colonial liberals had agitated for the ending of convict transportation and the advent of responsible government.[20] After these liberal reforms had been achieved and the early conservatives defeated, colonial liberals split into factions, with most politicians describing themselves as 'liberal' regardless of their political beliefs.[21] This liberal orthodoxy would be

---

18 George Reid in *Commonwealth Parliamentary Debates*, Vol. 49, pp.1145-57; *SMH*, Tuesday 14 March 1905, pp.5-6.
19 See Bruce Smith, *Liberty and Liberalism: a protest against the growing tendency toward undue interference by the State with individual liberty, private enterprise, and the rights of property*, Melbourne: G. Robertson, 1887.
20 H. V. Evatt, *Liberalism in Australia: An historical sketch of Australian politics down to the year 1915*, Sydney: the Law Book Co. of Australia, 1918, p.77.
21 Geoffrey Bolton, 'Henry (later Sir Henry) Parkes', in David Clune and Ken Turner, *The*

challenged in the late 1880's by the rise of interventionist ideologies, most notably protectionism. Protectionism would soon be followed by the rise of the Labor Party, and the period between the late 1880's and the First World War would be one of political flux, when the ideological dividing lines that have largely endured until the present day would be determined.

When the rise of protection heralded a debate over the 'fiscal issue', George Reid quickly joined the Free-Trade side that, in New South Wales at least, claimed to be the inheritors of the colonial liberal tradition. New South Wales Free-Traders portrayed themselves as the defenders of liberalism against the aristocratic rural supporters of protection.[22] Reid himself denounced protection in distinctly liberal terms, arguing that an attack on free-trade was the first step in a government assault on freedom to achieve particular ends.[23] Debate over the fiscal issue would still be raging when Reid began his anti-socialist campaign.

Although the tariff was the main political issue in late nineteenth century Australia, there were those who were expressing a liberal ideology that stood for more than freedom of trade. Bruce Smith's *Liberty and Liberalism* published in 1887 presented a distinctly liberal small government ideology that opposed the extension of state power. The fact that this book was published before the rise of the Labor Party shows that Australian small government liberalism is not inherently 'reactionary,' although the book was responding to the rise of 'social liberalism' in 1880s Victoria. Reid's five free-trade essays, published in 1875, had also expressed a liberal ideology, and when he became Premier in 1894 he began translating his liberal beliefs into practical politics. While he introduced free-trade in New South Wales, he also made the public service more efficient through his Public Service Act and introduced necessary taxation to make up for falling land sales revenue.[24] Reid fought the un-elected Legislative Council and opposed the local option

---

Premiers of New South Wales 1856-2005, Sydney: The Federation Press, 2006. See also Peter Loveday and Allan Martin, *Parliament, Factions and Parties: The First Thirty Years of Responsible Government in New South Wales 1856-1889*, Melbourne: Melbourne University Press, 1966.
22 See George Reid, *Five Free Trade Essays*, Melbourne: Gordon & Gotch, 1875.
23 W.G. McMinn, *George Reid*, Carlton: Melbourne University Press, 1989, p.50.
24 W.G. McMinn, *George Reid*, pp.107-118.

prohibition for which some of his protestant supporters yearned.[25] He also fought for a more liberal and democratic Commonwealth constitution, forever earning himself the title of Yes-No Reid by refusing to commit to a document that he saw as far from ideal.[26]

While Reid's successful Premiership was an exercise in 'positive' liberalism, events were taking place that would create the distinctly defensive anti-socialist liberalism. The most important of these developments was the rise of the Labor Party. This new Party had first won seats in the 1891 election, and their members formed a significant minority in parliament, though this was hampered by early splits that saw their parliamentary leader, Joseph Cook, leave the Party in 1894.[27] Reid's time as Premier was built on Labor Party support but their illiberal methods had begun to worry him. The first thing that made liberals uneasy about the Labor Party was the introduction of the pledge, which committed its members to voting according to the will of caucus. Control by caucus was an aberration to nineteenth century liberals who held strong individualist convictions, and when it was introduced many Labor members, including Cook, left their Party and joined Reid.[28] While the pledge was viewed as illiberal, Reid also saw the Labor Party's increasing dogmatism as incompatible with practical politics. During his premiership Labor scuttled Reid's Local Government bill, which they supported in principle, because they could not get every clause they wanted inserted into the act.[29]

W.G. McMinn has argued that the origins of the anti-socialist campaign lay in Reid's dealings with Labor during his time as Premier.[30] Such sentiment is misguided. While his time as Premier certainly had a negative effect on Reid's attitude towards Labor, it was their changing policy priorities which truly sparked his hatred. Reid had allied with Labor when he felt they were both fighting aristocratic privileges. It was

---

25 Ibid, pp.112-143.
26 See L. F. Crisp, *George Houstoun Reid: Federation Father. Federal Failure?* Canberra: SOCPAC printery, 1979.
27 John Rickard, 'Sir Joseph Cook', in Michelle Grattan (ed.), *Australian Prime Ministers*, Sydney: New Holland Publishers, 2000, p.93.
28 John Rickard, 'Sir Joseph Cook'.
29 George Reid, *My Reminiscences*, London: Cassell & Co. Ltd., 1917, pp113-4.
30 McMinn, *George Reid*, p.122.

when Labor began to fight for privileges to be given to unions that Reid developed an ideological opposition to his former allies.[31] The main cause of the anti-socialist campaign was the support of a large and growing section of the Labor Party for the 'socialist objective'. This growing support would manifest itself in the 1905 Queensland Labor Party conference's adoption of the objective of nationalising 'the means of production, distribution and exchange'.[32] The explicit desire to make Australia socialist expressed by this objective raised the ire of those whose liberal beliefs made them reject the extension of state power. The New South Wales Labor Party conference adopted the milder objective of the 'collective ownership of monopolies, and the extension of the industrial and economic functions of the state'.[33] In July the interstate Party conference adopted the New South Wales objective despite protests from Victoria and Queensland that this did not go far enough.[34] While anti-socialist liberals found this milder goal objectionable in itself, they also felt that it was simply a cover for the Labor Party's more extreme goals.[35]

Since the anti-socialist campaign grew out of a rejection of the 'nationalisation of the means of production, distribution and exchange' it was inherently liberal in its ideological outlook. Reid was not fighting the Labor Party because they were pursuing legislation supposedly for the benefit of the 'working class', he was fighting the Labor Party because they wanted to create an all-powerful state that was the antithesis of classical liberalism. Judith Brett has argued that Reid saw politics in terms of class divisions, curiously justifying her position with a quote in which Reid makes no mention of class.[36] The evidence suggests quite the opposite, as he had fought with the Labor Party against the Legislative Council, arguably the upholder of whatever little existed of a class system in New South Wales. Reid's anti-socialist campaign would be a

---

31 'Mr Reid in Sydney', *SMH* Tuesday 14 March 1905 pp5-6.
32 Quoted in Ross McMullin, *The Light On The Hill: The Australian Labor Party 1891-1991*, Melbourne: Oxford University Press, 1991, p.55.
33 Quoted in ibid, p.56.
34 Ibid, p.57.
35 'Final Speech at Maitland', *SMH* Friday 26 May 1905, p.7.
36 Brett, *Australian Liberals and the Moral Middle Class*, p.20.

campaign against class-based legislation and parties, that rejected trade union privileges and supported individualism and private enterprise.[37] In this articulation of liberalism we can see the origins of the beliefs supported by most in the modern Liberal Party. Importantly while rejecting a large and despotic state, it does not specify a distinct limit for government intervention. At the time this ambiguity was meant to help unite liberals in a moment of perceived crisis, today this ambiguity helps the 'broad church' stay together.

The anti-socialist campaign began in early 1905 when Reid was Prime Minister. The 1903 election had produced a parliament in which the Free-Traders, Protectionists and Labor all had roughly equal representation. The political turmoil that this election result produced had seen the fall of the Deakin and Watson administrations before Reid finally gained power in an alliance with some of the Protectionists. The need for Protectionist support meant that Reid could not pursue free-trade policies and had to adopt a 'fiscal truce'. With the tariff issue temporarily off the table Reid refocused his rhetoric against the Labor Party and its growing association with socialism. In doing this Reid was following the lead of Joseph Carruthers who, once becoming leader of the Liberal and Reform Party in 1902, had made socialism one of the main issues in New South Wales politics after federation had removed the fiscal issue from the State arena.[38] Importantly, Archdale Parkhill, who had played a large part in orchestrating Carruthers' 1904 election victory, would be given a central role in organising Reid's anti-socialist campaign.[39]

While Reid's shift in focus may seem like political opportunism, by advocating the anti-socialist cause Reid was forever abandoning any chance of trying to utilise Labor support as he had in New South Wales. When it is considered that he was operating in a three-party system where Deakin's refusal to be a part of cabinet made the Free-Trade Protectionist alliance seem highly unlikely to last, Reid was actually sacrificing future political opportunities by embarking on his anti-socialist campaign.

---

37 'Mr Reid in Sydney', *SMH* Tuesday 14 March 1905, pp.5-6; 'Mr Reid in Sydney', *SMH*, Monday 1 May 1905, p.5.
38 Michael Hogan, 'Introduction', in *Joseph Carruthers: A Lifetime in Conservative Politics*, Michael Hogan (ed.), (Sydney: UNSW Press Ltd. 2005), p.8.
39 Parkhill to Carruthers, 29/11/1906, Carruthers Papers, ML MSS 1638/28, p.145.

Like many Free-Trade liberals, Reid had been developing an ideological opposition to Labor's caucus and dogma for a long time, and this meant that he was able to bring to his new cause the same level of conviction with which he had once advocated free-trade. Reid's new focus would soon be vindicated when the Queensland Labor Party adopted the socialist objective, making the Labor Party appear to many liberals as a real threat to the freedoms they enjoyed. The anti-socialist campaign thus predated Labor's adoption of the socialist objective, although a significant group of the Party's members had already begun to openly advocate socialism.

Reid spent most of early 1905 touring the country preaching his liberal anti-socialist message. The themes he discussed in his speeches give us a clear insight into his conception of anti-socialism and its roots in his liberal beliefs. Reid's first major speech of the anti-socialist campaign was delivered in Sydney in March. In it Reid argued that 'just as he stood up, and fought the financiers, squatters, and capitalists of New South Wales to a finish, in order to establish a fair system of taxation, so now, in the name of democracy and in the principle of treating every man upon broad principles of common fairness and equality, and in the same old principle of political liberty, he had now to fight the trades unions of Australia'.[40] Reid's opposition to trade union privileges was a key theme of many of his speeches. He believed that legislation advocated by Labor that forced or pressured people into joining unions broke with the liberal ideal of freedom of association. Reid was not opposed to the existence of trade unions, but he was opposed to their politicisation and had tried to stop them from donating to political parties.[41] This opposition to the excessive political influence of trade unions, rather than to their existence, continues to be an important theme of Liberal Party discourse.

In a speech at Rockhampton, Reid attacked the Conciliation and Arbitration Act for disadvantaging non-unionists, even though he had helped pass the bill, because he felt that it went against the principle of

---

40 'Mr Reid in Sydney', *SMH* Tuesday 14 March 1905, pp.5-6.
41 McMinn, *George Reid*, p.208.

equality that underpinned 'British justice'.[42] Reid's defence of 'British justice' gives an important insight into his liberal beliefs and their relationship to a concept of equality. Reid believed in equality before the law, but not in socialism's equality of outcomes. For Reid equality of outcomes was essentially unfair as it reduced 'the march of the nation to the pace of the slowest and weakest'.[43] Reid's speeches show that he equated liberalism with opportunity; hence he felt that socialism was inherently illiberal partly because it destroyed opportunity. The recent Liberal Party campaign slogan 'hope, reward, opportunity', suggests that Reid's beliefs still resonate.

In many of his speeches Reid argued that socialistic equality would destroy human enterprise. In a speech to the Women's Liberal League he lamented that 'it would be a melancholy day for the human race when the incentives to develop human industry and genius were gone'.[44] The idea that private enterprise inspires creativity and productivity is a key neo-liberal belief. An interesting thing about Reid and the anti-socialist campaign was his ability to span the divide of liberal thought. At the same time that he was arguing the merits of private enterprise he was also acknowledging an important role for the state.[45] This approach reflected his pragmatism and also his need to appease small government ideological liberals like Bruce Smith and more interventionist liberals like Alfred Deakin. These competing liberal outlooks have always been present in the Liberal Party of Australia and anti-socialism's ability to accommodate both has helped ensure its enduring legacy. Importantly though there were levels of government intervention that even Reid's tactful ambiguity could not accept. Fiercely interventionist 'liberals' like Isaac Isaacs did not join the campaign and would ultimately not be part the Liberal Party. The demise of John Gorton as Prime Minister in 1971 is testament to the fact that even during the firmly Keynesian era there were limits to the amount of intervention and centralisation the Liberal Party would accept.

Although Reid's liberal anti-socialism would form the ideological basis

---

42 'The Prime Minister's Tour', *Brisbane Courier*, Thursday 8 June 1905, p.5.
43 'Prime Minister at Adelaide', *SMH*, Thursday 27 April 1905, p.7.
44 'Speech by Prime Minister', *SMH*, Tuesday 2 May 1905, p.7.
45 'Prime Minister at Perth', *SMH*, Wednesday 19 April 1905, p.7.

of the Commonwealth Liberal Party and eventually the Liberal Party of Australia, it is important to note that not all of his rhetorical constructs have endured. During a tour of regional New South Wales religion was brought into the anti-socialist controversy. In response to attempts by a number of Labor Party members to portray socialism as an extension of Christianity, Reid attacked what he felt were the inherent contradictions of such an association. Reid argued that free will was a gift from God that socialists were trying to constrain through the extension of the state.[46] He also believed that charity should be given freely and that by trying to use legislation as a means of charity the socialists were robbing charity of its moral value.[47] When Reid returned to Sydney he continued his critique of 'Christian socialism'. In a speech at Newtown Reid continued to develop his argument that the socialist state would destroy charity; 'the moment man is driven, even to do the best action in the world, by the force of the law, by compulsion, the merit of charity, the merit of religion, the merit of humanity is destroyed'.[48] He distinguished between socialism that relied on the state and Christianity which 'seeks to work by the love and voluntary sacrifice and good will of the people'.[49] Reid also tried to associate socialism with atheism, quoting Freidrich Engels 'we have simply done with God' and other statements by prominent socialists.[50] This religious detour in Reid's anti-socialist discourse reflects the historical and cultural circumstances of the anti-socialist campaign. In the early 1900's Australian society was far more religious than it is today and though some Liberal Party members may still agree with Reid's attacks on Christian socialism it is difficult to imagine a modern Liberal leader bringing religion into a political debate so audaciously.

While Reid was developing his anti-socialist ideas, some of his supporters were beginning to criticise him for not going far enough in advocating small government liberalism. Bruce Smith called on Reid to end his campaign of 'passive resistance' to socialism's spread and instead

---

46 'Something About Christian Socialism', *SMH*, Wednesday 24 May 1905, p.7.
47 Ibid.
48 'Mr Reid at Newtown', *SMH*, Saturday 3 June 1905, p.12.
49 Ibid.
50 Ibid.

to actively repeal the 'socialist measures of the last four years'.[51] He refused to attend a meeting of New South Wales anti-socialist members of parliament organised by Reid.[52] Smith also publicly criticised the White Australia policy, which Reid supported despite criticising the impact its implementation was having on immigration levels.[53] Smith's criticisms forced Reid to distance himself from the rogue member, stating publicly that 'there has never been any close political sympathy between Mr Bruce Smith and myself'.[54]

It is easy to see why Reid would be uncomfortable with Smith utilising his liberal right to disagree with his leader. Smith's attitudes towards the White Australia policy and the Conciliation and Arbitration Act called for a debate on the limits of government intervention within a liberal antisocialist framework. Smith was calling for a small government approach that rejected not only the 'nationalisation of the means of production, distribution and exchange' but also much of what he saw as the 'socialist' interventionist legislation that had already been passed by the fledgling federal parliament. This included many pieces of legislation that had been passed by the former Protectionist government, the supporters of which Reid was now trying to keep on side. This was exactly the kind of divisive internal debate that Reid wanted to avoid as he struggled to present a united liberal front for the next election.

Despite these criticisms Smith was eventually reconciled with the 'broad church' of Reid's anti-socialism. Accepting that the socialist objective represented a tangible threat against which liberals should unite, Smith helped establish four branches of the Australian Liberal League in his electorate.[55] He also delivered a number of campaign speeches in support of anti-socialism and debated Labor leader Chris Watson through the pages of the *Sydney Morning Herald*.[56] Bruce Smith's example shows that even in its developmental stages, liberal anti-socialism was able to accommodate a wide difference of opinion. The ability of this

---

51 'Mr Bruce Smith and the Government Policy', *SMH*, Friday 7 April 1905, p.7.
52 Ibid.
53 'Anti-Socialism', *SMH*, Thursday 18 May 1905, p.6.
54 'Summary', *SMH*, Monday 1 May 1905, p.1.
55 'Anti-Socialism', *SMH*, Wednesday 14 June 1905, p.6.
56 'Socialism, reply to Mr Bruce Smith', *SMH*, Friday 9 June 1905, p.8.

ideology to unite liberals with varying beliefs has helped it endure as the ideological cornerstone of the Liberal Party of Australia through both the Keynesian and neo-liberal eras.

The first stage of the anti-socialist campaign ended in July 1905 when Alfred Deakin withdrew his support for Reid and the Reid-McLean government fell. Deakin's withdrawal of support is a key moment in the history of Australian liberalism. As Reid was quick to remind people for the rest of the campaign, Deakin had denounced the Labor Party and its caucus and had agreed to a fiscal truce.[57] In light of these denunciations the question must be asked, why did Deakin wreck the Reid government and bid for Labor support? Deakin justified his position by labelling Reid and the Anti-Socialists as a negative Party, but it seems unlikely that this was his main motivation. After all Deakin argued that the Labor Party advocated 'an extension of the powers of the state which might threaten to absorb many of the great industrial functions of the community', hence he himself had a 'negative' reaction, at least to the extent of Labor's programme of nationalisation.[58] The real reason that Deakin abandoned Reid was that he felt that 'the Anti-Socialists are absolutely opposed to protection', despite Reid's repeated assurances about a fiscal truce.[59] Deakin felt a fiscal truce was inadequate and wanted protection even if that meant making a deal with the Labor Party that he had so recently attacked.

The political circumstances of Deakin's choice of protection over anti-socialism are of central importance in understanding the historical legacy of his decision. Deakin abandoned anti-socialism at a time when the Queensland Labor Party was advocating the 'nationalisation of the means of production, distribution and exchange' and there were strong moves to have that policy inserted into the national Labor Party platform. The 'nationalisation of the means of production, distribution and exchange' is the most socialist policy ever advocated by the Australian Labor Party and would have resulted in the effective establishment of a communist state had the objective been carried out. As we have already

---

57 'The Labour Conference', *SMH*, Monday 17 July 1905, p.7.
58 'Alfred Deakin at Adelaide', *SMH*, Friday 30 March 1906, p.5.
59 Ibid.

seen Deakin himself had acknowledged the threat to liberalism that at least the scope of this objective represented, but he still decided not to join with Reid in presenting Labor with a united liberal anti-socialist front.

Because Deakin chose protection over anti-socialism in these circumstances it seems unfitting that he is so often considered a founding father of the Liberal Party. While for much of its history the Liberal Party has supported protection, for all of its history it has supported anti-socialism. The Liberal Party of Australia is, despite debates about what this might mean in practice, fundamentally an anti-socialist party. Deakin's actions in July 1905 show that fundamentally he was a protectionist not an anti-socialist; consequently his guiding political principles do not resonate in the modern Liberal Party in the way that those of his lesser-known rival George Reid do.

Despite Deakin's rejection of anti-socialism many historians may still argue that Deakin is a more important figure for Australian liberalism than Reid because of Reid's supposed 'conservatism' and Deakin's 'liberalism'. Reid is often portrayed as a sort of anti-Deakin, someone who was either completely laissez-faire or as Brett argued a believer in class divisions.[60] In this way he is the victim not just of a long Victorian domination of the Liberal Party, but also his own failure to leave us a useful collection of papers so that we are often forced to view this period of history through Deakin's eyes.[61] As this paper has already shown however Reid's anti-socialism was fundamentally an extension of his colonial liberalism. Reid like Deakin had held government with Labor support, though when Reid did it the Labor Party had not adopted the socialist objective. In his anti-socialist campaign Reid was attacking despotic big government and union compulsion in purely liberal terms. After July 1905 Reid would have to continue to develop his liberal anti-socialist ideas in opposition and without the support of the Protectionists.

Reid used the 1905 parliamentary session to portray the 'socialism' of the legislation being introduced by the new Labor-supported

---

60 Brett, *Australian Liberals and the Moral Middle Class*, p.20.
61 See for example Alfred Deakin, *The Federal Story*, J. A. La Nauze (ed.), Melbourne: Melbourne University Press, 1963.

Protectionist government. The main object of his attacks was the union label provision of the Trade Marks Bill. This provision allowed a union label to be attached to any product as having been produced by union labour under 'liveable conditions'.[62] In order to be eligible for the label all of the workers employed by the manufacturer of the product had to be union members. Reid argued that this was an attempt to pressure people into joining unions or to threaten non-union jobs, as employers would seek the benefit of attaching the union label to their products.[63] In parliament Reid used fiery rhetoric to portray his message; "of all attempts to create monopoly, I think the most cruel is the attempt of working men to create a privilege and a monopoly against their fellow industrialists".[64] Reid's attacks were meant to show the urgency of the socialist threat. If the Labor party could pass legislation that was 'socialist' when it was not even in power the consequences of a Labor government would, according to Reid, be dire. Reid's logic followed that the only way to stop socialist legislation was to vote for his Anti-Socialists, not the Protectionists who allowed Labor to exercise power without responsibility.[65] The debates over the Trade Marks Bill echo recent Liberal criticisms that the Greens exercised power without responsibility in their influence over the former Labor government. The historical importance of these debates lies not with these analogies however but with Reid's attempts to translate his liberal anti-socialism into a policy position. It was this conversion of ideology into practical politics that would eventually allow anti-socialism to remain relevant once the initial threat of the socialist objective had begun to subside.

In the meantime though, the anti-socialist controversy was still very much alive. As such in early April 1906 a debate was organised between Reid and William Holman on 'The Principle of Socialism as Defined in the Objective and Platform of the Labor Party'.[66] The debate was an opportunity for Reid to organise all his various critiques of socialism into one unified argument. In essence Reid's argument was that socialism

---

62 *Commonwealth Parliamentary Debates*, Vol. XXV, p.588.
63 Ibid, p.591.
64 Ibid.
65 *Commonwealth Parliamentary Debates*, Vol. XXVII, p.2714.
66 McMinn, *George Reid*, p.235.

destroyed man's enterprising spirit, hurt the economy and converted "a condition of liberty and free choice…into the condition of perpetual official authority and subjection".[67] The debate also saw Reid portray his ideal alternative to the socialist state. Reid defined the ideal state as "A community of highly educated men and women enjoying the fullest measure of personal liberty, but under no compulsion to do their duty to their neighbours and to the State".[68] He went on to describe the ideal government as "a government whose power is ever exercised to improve the opportunities of the people and never exercised to interfere with their personal liberty so long as they abstained from wrongdoing".[69]

Reid's positive ideological constructions of the ideal state and government were largely a response to attacks by Deakin, which labelled anti-socialism a "necklace of negatives".[70] They were also a response to Bruce Smith's discourse on liberalism, which forced Reid to define his attitude towards the role of the state. In defining his beliefs Reid allowed "the doing by the government of every necessary and good thing which people cannot do for themselves, or which smooths the path of private enterprise".[71] Reid's ideological construction thus allowed an active role for government as long as this role did unnecessarily damage private enterprise. This statement could be used to foreshadow the Keynesian liberalism of the Menzies era, though it seems highly unlikely that Reid, who was schooled in classical liberalism, would have supported policies that were as interventionist as those that Keynes advocated. At the same time, those who object to Keynesianism could also use Reid's construction, as they would argue that Keynesian policies hinder rather than smooth "the path of private enterprise".

Reid's definition steered clear of explaining what exactly "people cannot do for themselves" or what level of government involvement to "smooth the path of private enterprise" would be tolerated within anti-socialism. Although this lack of explanation allowed Reid to keep his 'broad church' together, it was not merely an act of political evasion.

---

67 'Mr Reid in Reply', *SMH*, Wednesday 4 April 1906, p.9.
68 Ibid.
69 Ibid.
70 'Prime Minister's Policy', *Argus*, Monday 26 March 1906, p.9.
71 'Mr Reid in Reply', *SMH*, Wednesday 4 April 1906, p.9.

Reid had always been a pragmatist not a dogmatist and his definition left him room to manoeuvre.[72] It is often said that ideology has played a comparatively small role in Australian politics, and it is interesting to note that even during what was perhaps the most ideological period of Australian political history, the Anti-Socialists were being led by a pragmatist who did not impose a dogmatic interpretation of liberalism on his followers. The 'broad church' model of Australian liberalism, laid down by Reid's anti-socialism did not however represent a playing down of ideology. Ideology was of central importance to the anti-socialist campaign and has remained very important to Australian politics. Even in Australia, it is belief in particular ideology that makes individuals join a political party and which motivates, to some extent at least, all but the most careerist of politicians. What Australian politics generally lacks, certainly on the Liberal side of politics, is not ideology but dogmatism. The amount of political flexibility exercised by Australian political leaders does not show that they don't believe strongly in an ideology, it shows that that ideology is not dogmatic and is open to interpretation. 'Liberalism' itself is an extremely subjective term, Reid realised this and that was why he took pains to make sure liberal anti-socialism was an inclusive ideology, not an exclusive one.

Reid spent much of 1906 travelling the country on campaign tours that were even more extensive than those on which he had embarked in 1905. In order to facilitate this campaigning Reid was absent from parliament for long periods of time. Reid was politically able to afford these absences because of the competency of his deputy Joseph Cook. In his memoirs Reid wrote that "the able and devoted services of Mr Joseph Cook, as deputy leader of the opposition, were the main factors in making my position tolerable. Had he been less able, or less loyal, or less devoted than he was, a leadership so long and so often suspended as mine could not have lasted for a single session".[73] Joseph Cook's time as deputy opposition leader would have a major impact on the history of liberalism in Australia. Cook used his time in parliament to hone his political skills as an advocate of anti-socialism. It was these political

---

72 For examples of Reid's political pragmatism see McMinn, *George Reid*.
73 George Reid, *My Reminiscences*, p.255.

skills that would allow Cook to win the 1913 election at the head the Commonwealth Liberal Party, a feat that Deakin failed to achieve. It was the 1913 election that produced the first elected Liberal majority government at a federal level and cemented the position of liberal anti-socialism in Australian political culture.

Reid delivered his election manifesto on the twenty third of October, more than a month before the 1906 election. In it Reid dismissed claims that he was "reactionary and conservative" insisting that anti-socialism was inherently "liberal and democratic".[74] Connecting anti-socialism with a liberalism inherited from the pre-Federation period, Reid claimed that "our policy has always been directed against monopoly and privilege, in every shape and form".[75] Reid's middle ground approach that positioned liberalism as a bulwark against the use of government for the privilege of any class would be echoed by Menzies in his espousal of liberal ideals. In 1943 Menzies would take Reid's middle ground arguing that liberalism stood against both communism and the extreme right.[76] Reid's manifesto also attacked Labor's taxes and Deakin's tariff protection for increasing the cost of living and placing burdens on the poor.[77] The idea that the poor are worse off under an interventionist government with high taxes and a poor economy is something that would be supported by neo-liberals and many within the modern Liberal Party. Indeed the current Liberal Party built its recent election campaign on attacking the increase in cost of living pressures that had occurred under the Labor government.

Reid made a final appeal to voters on election day, the twelfth of December. Through the pages of the *Sydney Morning Herald* he argued that "the real choice is one between socialism and liberalism, between force and freedom".[78] Since voting was non-compulsory, Reid urged people to get out and vote, keen to ensure that the Labor Party's ability to mobilise its supporter base would not cost him the election.[79] Finally he appealed "to all lovers of freedom, to every believer in free, industrial

---

74 'Liberal Manifesto', *SMH*, Wednesday 24 October 1906, p.9.
75 'Liberal Manifesto', *SMH*, Wednesday 24 October 1906, p.9.
76 'Liberal system in politics', *SMH*, Saturday 30 October 1943, p.11.
77 'Liberal Manifesto', *SMH*, Wednesday 24 October 1906, p.9.
78 'Mr Reid's final appeal', *SMH*, Wednesday 12 December 1906, p.9.
79 Ibid.

opportunities for all, to stand side by side with me in resisting the avalanche of selfishness and socialistic tyranny which threatens to overwhelm the freest, brightest, most loyal, and progressive community on the face of the earth to-day".[80] In hindsight it is easy to dismiss rhetoric like this and label Reid's anti-socialist campaign as a 'scare campaign'. Indeed many political historians have done so.[81] Such assertions are anachronistic. Although the Labor Party never carried out the "nationalisation of the means of production, distribution and exchange", at the time this outcome seemed a distinct possibility. Indeed, it is likely that one of the reasons the Labor Party turned away from extreme policies like the socialist objective was because George Reid and others were successful in highlighting the perceived dangers of socialism to the electorate; thus the campaign fulfilled its main goal of preventing a the establishment of a socialist Australia.[82] Such a possibility is seldom acknowledged by Labor historians, who prefer to leave the historical agency over the direction of their party firmly in the hands of its members.

While Reid made his appeal in the *Sydney Morning Herald*, his old political ally, New South Wales Premier Joseph Carruthers, issued an appeal "to the federal electors of New South Wales", in the *Daily Telegraph*.[83] Carruthers supported Reid's election and anti-socialist ideology, arguing that "the state's prosperity today is not owing to the laws of parliament, but to the enterprise of the people".[84] He appealed "As a native-born Australian and the son of a working man, and as one who has risen from the lowest rung of the ladder to almost the highest position in the land, I feel that the incentive to the exercise of ability and industry lies in the encouragement of individual merit under liberalism rather than in the levelling down of men under socialism".[85] Carruthers'

---

80 Ibid.
81 See McMullin, *Light On The Hill*, p.55; Michael Hogan, '1907', in Michael Hogan and David Clune (eds.), *The People's Choice: Electoral Politics in 20th Century New South Wales Volume 1 1901-1927*, Sydney: Parliament of New South Wales and the University of Sydney, 2001, p.75.
82 For an example of a Labor leader fighting for the removal of the socialist objective explicitly because it was electorally damaging, see H.V. Evatt, *Australian Labour Leader: The Story of W. A. Holman and the Labour Movement*, Sydney: Angus & Robertson, 1954, p.122.
83 *Daily Telegraph* clipping, 11/12/1906, Carruthers papers, ML MSS 1638/115.
84 Ibid.
85 Ibid.

sentiment is important as it shows another highly prominent New South Wales colonial liberal who had undergone the same political evolution as Reid had. This helps to suggest that anti-socialism was a natural extension of liberalism for such men and not a political volte-face by Reid. After the election, despite Carruthers' very open backing of Reid and Archdale Parkhill's prominent organisational role, there would be a lot of consternation over the suggestion that Carruthers' state Liberal Party had not done enough to help their federal counterparts.[86] Though in New South Wales they shared a common liberal anti-socialist ideology, Liberal federal and state organisations were largely separate institutions at this point in time, putting them at a major disadvantage compared to their Labor opponents.

The 1906 election took place on the twelfth of December. Once the votes were counted it was clear that Reid had not won a majority in his own right. Despite a significant drop in Protectionist support the Deakin government would endure with Labor backing. In a newspaper interview given two days after the election Reid claimed that with the Anti-Socialists and the Protectionists a majority of the members returned to the house were opposed to socialism.[87] Joseph Carruthers defended Reid's results, pointing to Senate results to argue that the three-party system, sectarianism and voter apathy had cost him dearly.[88] Voter turnout was low, just 51.48%, perhaps because the three-party system and the competing socialism and fiscal issues had confused voters (there were many independent protectionists who were essentially anti-socialist protectionists, highlighting the fact that the two issues complicated the political scene).[89]

The Anti-Socialist M.P. Dugald Thomson argued that if the electorates were of equal size in terms of population the Anti-Socialists would have won three more seats in New South Wales.[90] Using Senate results to estimate results in uncontested seats Thomson claimed that in New

---

86 *Daily Telegraph* clipping, 24/12/1906, Carruthers papers, ML MSS 1638/115.
87 'Mr Reid's views', *SMH*, Friday 14 December 1906, p.5.
88 *Daily Telegraph* clipping, 14/12/1906, Carruthers papers, ML MSS 1638/115.
89 Colin Hughes and B.D. Graham, *A Handbook of Australian Government and Politics 1890-1964*, Canberra: ANU Press 1968, p.297.
90 'Minority rule', *SMH*, Wednesday 19 December 1906, p.9.

South Wales the Anti-Socialists received 186 254 votes, Labor received 137 334 votes and the Protectionists received 33,971.[91] According to these figures the Anti-Socialists received more than half the votes in New South Wales yet they won only eleven of twenty-six seats. This discrepancy between the votes the Anti-Socialists received and the seats they won was apparent throughout the country, as the Anti-Socialists received 38.17% of votes for the House of Representatives, yet only won 34.67% of the seats (not including the independent protectionists who generally supported Reid).[92] These figures also show that the Anti-Socialists received the most votes of any party, yet the Protectionists, who received less than half the votes of either of the other major parties, and whose proportion of the vote had dropped significantly on both occasions that Deakin had lead them to an election, managed to retain their grip on government.[93] In the Senate the Anti-Socialists received 46.53% of the vote, suggesting that a large number of people who voted for a Protectionist or an independent protectionist in the House voted for the Anti-Socialists in the Senate.[94] This may mean that people with anti-socialist beliefs often voted for sitting Protectionist members, or that many people who wanted a Protectionist government voted for the Anti-Socialists in the upper house in the hope of blocking the passage of 'socialist' legislation.

Reid failed to win the 1906 election because a number of competing political issues prevented him from making the election the referendum on socialism that he wanted it to be. Chief among these competing issues was protection, with Deakin's intransigence preventing the two ostensibly liberal groups from uniting. Despite a noticeable drop in Protectionist support, Deakin was able to pass the protective tariff for which he had abandoned Reid. Even though the Deakin government survived the 1906 election, the anti-socialist campaign had been successful in creating a major shift in Australian political discourse.[95] It became clear that after

---

91 Ibid.
92 Hughes and Graham, *Handbook of Australian Government and Politics*, p.296.
93 Ibid, pp.286-296.
94 Ibid, p.297.
95 See Zachary Gorman, 'Debating a Tiger Cub: The Anti-Socialist Campaign', Honours Thesis, University of Sydney, 2012.

the tariff had been passed Australian politics would realign into a two-party system divided over the issue of socialism. The 1909 fusion of the Protectionist and Anti-Socialist Parties saw this realignment eventuate. Having passed his protectionist tariff, Alfred Deakin took up the anti-socialist cause that he had abandoned in 1905. The electorate did not forget Deakin's previous lukewarm attitude towards anti-socialism and the 1910 election resulted in a crushing defeat for the new Commonwealth Liberal Party. In the aftermath of this defeat Reid's liberal anti-socialism may have been consigned to the historical dustbin had it not been for the election of Reid's former deputy, Joseph Cook, as the new leader of the CLP. Preaching the political ideology that had been developed by Reid, Cook won the 1913 election cementing the liberal anti-socialist/labor political divide that has endured until the present day.

Most historians see the 1909 fusion as the key moment in the creation of the Australian political divide and there have been two books entirely devoted to the study of the fusion.[96] The creation of the Commonwealth Liberal Party was not a new beginning for Australian politics however; it was the result of the political *fait accompli* the anti-socialist campaign had created for the Protectionist Party. Reid's great efforts to popularise anti-socialism combined with the Labor Party's own efforts in pushing the "nationalisation of the means of production, distribution and exchange", meant that the political debate was moving away from the Protectionists so that they faced fusion or political oblivion. Although Deakin's political gravitas meant that he would lead the new Commonwealth Liberal Party, its ideology was almost entirely inherited from Reid. Even its support for protection was in essence a recreation of the 'fiscal truce' as Deakin's tariff had already been put into law.

In light of these historical circumstances it seems that the modern Liberal Party's image of its history needs to be readjusted to acknowledge a greater role for Reid and a lesser role for Deakin than has previously been assumed. The origins of the modern Liberal Party lie in the liberal anti-socialist ideology Reid developed and espoused during the anti-socialist

---

[96] P. Loveday, A.W. Martin, and R.S. Parker (eds.), *The Emergence of the Australian Party System*, Sydney: Hale and Iremonger, 1977; Paul Strangio and Nick Dyrenfurth (eds.), *Confusion: The Making of the Australian Two-Party System*, Melbourne: Melbourne University Publishing, 2009.

campaign. This ideology is the unifying factor that ties the Keynesian, neo-liberal, wet liberal and conservative supporters together. Whatever their beliefs about what level of government intervention is ideal, almost all members of the Liberal Party think that there is a limit to the amount of government intervention that can be tolerated. The modern Liberal Party rejects excessive government manifested in high taxes and debt in the same way that Menzies rejected the excessive government of communism and fascism and in the way that Reid's liberal ideology made him reject the excessive and despotic nature of socialist government.

This paper does not mean to exaggerate Reid's role in creating a liberal anti-socialist ideology in Australia. As has already been noted, Bruce Smith was propagating small government liberalism before Reid was Premier. While Joseph Carruthers had used anti-socialism in his 1904 New South Wales election campaign, the Kyabram movement and Australian Women's National League were preaching an anti-socialist ideology in Victoria.[97] Although anti-socialist movements were emerging in Australia before 1905, it was Reid's campaign that popularised the issue. Reid's extensive tours of every state in the country began to break down the barriers that separated the independent political discourses of the newly federated states, helping to make socialism a truly 'national' political issue.[98]

Perhaps Reid's greatest ideological contribution to the anti-socialist liberalism that was emerging in the commonwealth was his accommodation of the 'broad church' of Australian liberalism. The internal conflicts within the Liberal Party of Australia do not date back to the merger of the so-called 'conservative' Anti-Socialist Party with the 'liberal' Protectionists; they were present at the very beginning when Reid first unfurled his 'anti-socialist banner'. George Reid was not, as has been suggested, the propagator of an almost laissez-faire free-trade ideology that was cannibalised by Victorians and re-emerged as a practically identical neo-liberal ideology under John Howard.[99] Although

---

[97] D.W. Rawson, 'Victoria', in Martin and Parker (eds.), *Emergence of the Australian Party System*, pp.90-91.
[98] Gorman, 'Debating a Tiger Cub: The Anti-Socialist Campaign', pp.7-69.
[99] Norman Abjorensen, 'Three Perspectives on John Howard: The Reid Legacy, NSW Exceptionalism and the Fulfilment of Liberal Prophecy', paper delivered at the John Howard

in practice Reid was certainly more small government than Deakin, and elements of his beliefs can easily be seen as an antecedents of Australian neo-liberalism, he created an anti-socialist ideological construction that avoided hard and fast definitions of what liberalism meant, allowing small government liberal ideologues and interventionist 'progressives' to unite in opposition to what they saw as the socialist threat. As well as a means of achieving unity, this ideological ambiguity was also a product of Reid's pragmatism. This pragmatism and ambiguity have remained present throughout the history of the Liberal Party of Australia, allowing the party to achieve many successes, perhaps at the expense of its ideological purity.

Decade Conference, Canberra, March 2006.

2

Liberalism, Conservatism and the Growth of Government in Australia

David Kemp

Introduction

This paper explores the relationship between liberal and conservative political thinking and the growth of government in Australia. It starts from the observation that the growth of the Australian state has gone through two distinct phases: an early expansion, as measured by spending, economic regulation, and direct state involvement in the economy and society, to become relatively one of the 'largest' of the democratic states up to 1930, followed by a second phase of readjustment which has left it, despite further growth after 2009, as relatively one of the 'smaller' less intrusive democratic states. The paper offers an interpretation of Australian political history, in which this readjustment of the state is explained by phases in the development of the liberal political tradition in Australia. It considers how this tradition has been expressed through political leaders and political parties, and the way in which they have responded to Australia's individualist culture, using expert policy analysis to counter special interest pressures. The paper concludes that the liberal ideas carried by political parties and high quality public policy analysis will be the key factors in the continuing rational adjustment of the state to fit with Australia's individualist values.

The Australian Case

Australia is a valuable case for the examination of the factors leading both to the growth of government and to its control. It has the advantage of being an example of a long-established liberal democracy which, very early in its history, developed a rapidly expanding government as a result of continent-wide imperial development ambitions and the humanitarian and religious ideals of a well-educated immigrant society.

The early democratic state in Australia rapidly became very expansive in its borrowing and spending on development works as a major element of Britain's imperial project. By the end of World War I this development state had been supplemented by far-reaching regulatory interventions, especially in the labour market and immigration, international trade, rural industries and in the enforcement of anti-competitive monopolistic practices. It made an early entry into income redistribution to provide an income security safety-net for the aged, sick (and later, unemployed). Its levels of government ownership of business enterprises, including rail, tramway and shipping, post and telecommunications, and gas and electricity, as well as banking, public education and health; and its social regulation to secure distinct gender roles and encourage church attendance, restrict alcohol and enforce sexual morality through censorship – all these taken together indicate a scale and scope of government more extensive than in almost any other liberal democratic state at the time.

By 1929 total government spending in Australia has been estimated to have reached around 33 per cent of GDP,[1] a level that, at that time, was possibly the highest in the western world. In the UK, government spending in 1929 was 24 per cent of GDP, while US government spending was around 11 per cent of GDP and Canada 13 per cent. The exceptional level of government spending was largely debt, rather than revenue – an indication of taxpayer resistance. Total public debt (Federal and State) by 1929 had reached 127.64 per cent of GDP.[100] Australia had the Western world's most regulated labour market through a system of compulsory arbitration of industrial disputes, and had, second only to the United States, the world's highest levels of tariff protection for domestic industry. Its immigration policy of White Australia excluded most coloured people. It had become, the economist E.O.G. Shann

---

100 Wray Vamplew (ed), *Australians: Historical Statistics*, Sydney: Fairfax, Syme & Weldon Associates, 1987, p.256.

wrote in 1930, 'a hermit nation', attempting to secure a high standard of living for all its white workers by closing itself to the world.[101]

Looking back from 2012 to, say, 1929, we can say that while government spending as a proportion of GDP, at around 35 percent of GDP, is around similar levels to that of eighty years before, its level relative to that of other democracies and its composition has changed markedly. Government spending in Australia is now at the lower, rather than the higher end, of practice in the democratic countries, comparing to the United States at 39 per cent, Canada 40 per cent, New Zealand 41 per cent, Germany 44 per cent, the UK at 47 and Sweden at 52 per cent.[102] While other states increased their spending, Australian governments restricted theirs. By 2007 the Federal government had reduced its public sector borrowing requirement to zero. Federal public sector debt has re-emerged following the global financial crisis, but remains at relatively low levels internationally.

The relative size of the government administration (as distinct from employees of government businesses) has also remained reasonably stable. In 1929 all Australian governments employed 14.7 per cent of the workforce. Today the figure is approximately 16 per cent. This puts Australia in the middle range of democracies, with Sweden twice as high (and the highest) at 32.3 per cent, while Canada is over 20 per cent, and Japan and Taiwan are under 10 per cent. Government employment in the United States as a proportion of the workforce is around the same level as in Australia.

Further, with limited exceptions such as motor vehicles, Australia has now become a free trading country with an economy open to international competition. Tariff walls have been dismantled, and only a tiny fraction of employment is now in trade-protected industries. The exchange rate now floats and the financial system is open to foreign banking. The highly regulated labour market had been considerably decentralised and freed up (though there has been some retrogression since 2007). Most

---

101 E.O.G. Shann, *Economic History of Australia*, Cambridge: Cambridge University Press, 1930.
102 Heritage Foundation, 2011 Index of Economic Freedom *Government expenditure as a percentage of GDP by country"*, *The Heritage Foundation: 2011 Index of Economic Freedom*. Retrieved from http://www.NationMaster.com/graph/gov_gov_spe_gov_exp_as_a_per_of_gdp-government-spending-expenditure-percentage-gdp

of the government business enterprises (including banks, airlines, and telecommunications) have been privatised and competition in some form reintroduced into the provision of power, posts, and transport. In the airline industry, originally drawn heavily into the regulatory net, including a government-owned airline, privatisation has eliminated government ownership and competition has vastly increased (though it is still not fully open). The detailed anti-competitive regulation of the rural industries has largely been dismantled (though debates continue over the co-ordinated marketing of some commodities).

As a qualitative measure of the relative extent of economic deregulation, the most recent ranking by the Heritage Foundation of the countries of the world by economic freedom has placed Australia (excepting only the city states of Hong Kong and Singapore) as economically the freest country in the world.[103]

This is a remarkable turn-around. Given the growth of government in other liberal democracies since the Second World War, it might have been predicted that the large Australian state of 1929 would become the foundation for an even larger one – that Australia might have led the way towards the minutely regulated society forecast for democracies by Alexis de Tocqueville.[104] At the very least, it might have been forecast that government in Australia would come to spend the proportion of national production in, say, a Sweden, or that its regulation of economic life might have progressed towards the levels experienced in Britain before Thatcher, or even in eastern Europe. Yet that did not happen.

To many Australian liberals the state is still too large – its taxes are too high, its regulatory interventions are too great, its administration is too large and inefficient, and it is too responsive to those who wish to restrict liberty to protect their own opinions and interests. The reversion of the Rudd-Gillard Labor-Greens alliance 2007-2013 to more traditional centralist/interventionist policies has heightened concern that continuing incremental movement towards de Tocqueville's minutely regulated society remains a risk. This may lead to further reform. Yet

---

103 Heritage Foundation, 2012 Index of Economic Freedom, http://www.heritage.org/index/ranking
104 Alexis de Tocqueville, *Democracy in America*, J.P. Mayer and Max Lerner, (eds.), George Lawrence (trans.), NY, Harper Collins, 1966 [1835].

on the whole there appears wide popular acceptance among Australians of their government's general scale and scope. How this will play out in the politics of coming decades remains to be seen, but what seems indisputable is that Australian democracy has shown a remarkable capacity to readjust and refashion its government in the light of experience and analysis and to resist to a significant extent the unceasing interest pressures for government to expand its activities.

This paper explores the politics associated with this historic readjustment, the role of liberal ideas and conservative attitudes and how they were brought to bear on policy. It concludes with some thoughts on the significance of this experience for the future.

Individualism and Collectivism in the Political and Popular Culture

The main outlines of the story of the expansion of the Australian state before the Great Depression are well known: the active, debt-financed, development state that, in pursuit of national industry became highly protectionist, quickly developed a policy tradition of government ownership of utilities and enterprises, and gave rise to a powerful union movement that pushed towards unprecedented 'state experiments' in the regulation of the labour market and industry. This state, in defence of the British settlement, largely closed its doors to immigrants from Asia and the Pacific, and as a result of external threat between 1914-1918 developed further exceptional regulation of rural industries, including licensing of entry to some industries and government-supervised marketing authorities.

It has been suggested that this surge of government activity expressed in some way a 'collectivism' in the Australian culture which distinguished Australia from the 'individualism' of the United States. This 'collectivism' has been traced to the dominance of the state during the convict period, and to the level of social-co-operation demanded by the Australian frontier. The rise of an exceptionally large trade union movement demanding more state action has also been seen as an expression of this culture. Yet when the attempt is made to link political and cultural ideas to the rapid expansion of government in Australia, there is a danger of circularity in assuming that expansive government necessarily reflects a 'collectivist' culture. The use of government itself was often described as 'collectivist', and such extensive use of government to control economic life could, with such a usage, properly be described as 'collectivist'. But the more interesting and important issue is whether this use was supported by a culture that could be described as dominated by collectivist values, and whether these were stronger than individualist values, and could be said to have driven the expansion of the state.

There were certainly advocates of collectivist values who were very influential in the Australia of the 1880s and 1890s. The most widely read collectivist writer in Australia at the time was probably the American Edward Bellamy, whose book *Looking Backward 2000-1887*[105] proposed an effectively communist, though middle class, society to replace private property and capitalism. "Bellamy's book was a revelation to the working classes. It sold by the hundred thousand, and few of that generation who claim to be readers at all, have failed to read it. It was the theme of conversation and debate in every workshop… The thoughtful readers of the working classes saw a new revelation", wrote J.D. Fitzgerald in his history of the rise of the Labor Party.[106]

The essence of such collectivism was the replacement of the pursuit of self-centred individual purposes with public purposes, which might involve a degree of 'compulsory co-operation' and self-denial, but in the interests of the greater good. Such collectivists argued that the pursuit of private purposes was 'selfish'. By 1890 the advocacy of a 'co-operative', as distinct from a 'competitive', society had become a prominent feature of both Australian and international political debate. The economist Alfred Marshall, at Cambridge, in his *Principles of Economics* (1890) thought that the term 'competition' – an economic process he thought essential to progress – should be replaced as a description of the workings of the liberal economy because of the negative connotations it had acquired. He suggested 'freedom of enterprise'.[107]

---

105 Edward Bellamy, *Looking Backward 2000-1887*, London: George Routledge & Sons Ltd., 1936 [1887].
106 J.D. Fitzgerald, *The Rise of the Australian Labor Party*, Sydney, 1915.
107 Alfred Marshall, *Principles of Economics, Vols. I & II*, Ninth (Variorum) Ed., C.W. Guillebaud (ed.), London: Macmillan & Co., 1920.

Not only trade union leaders such as W.G. Spence, but Liberals such as Samuel Griffith were contemplating how the more co-operative society could be brought into being, and the idea of voluntary co-operatives as an alternative to enterprises based on private property was widely discussed. Whether, given the element of compulsion being proposed by Bellamy, it could be said that his so-called 'co-operative society' was truly co-operative was a matter of dispute at the level of elite debate. The English social theorist Herbert Spencer distinguished the 'voluntary' co-operation of classical liberalism from the 'coerced' co-operation of Tory militarism and of the 'new' interventionist liberalism. Co-operation, he believed, could not be enforced by the state and still merit the description.

Alfred Deakin, a man who strongly believed in the use of government to correct social ills, doubted whether the ideal of the truly co-operative society as advocated by the collectivists could exist given human nature:

> State Socialism I fear only because of the weakness of the social idea in us. Run by selfishness, nothing could exceed the corruption likely to be bred under a system of State Socialism, but safeguarding this, I have no desire other than to extend the sphere of State interference and control.[108]

The fact that political activists were advocating the 'co-operative' society did not, however, mean that they were reflecting the cultural values of the wider population. If they were, and if the wider culture were significantly 'collectivist' in this sense, it is not easy to explain how this culture was compatible with the reversion of the Australian state to become one of the smaller governments of the Western world in the second half of the twentieth century. There are, indeed, good reasons for thinking that the explanation of the expansion of government in terms of 'collectivist' values is wrong, and that, far from reflecting such values, the rise of the Australian state was more the consequence of a powerfully and (often selfishly) *individualist* culture.

This is not in itself a novel suggestion. W.K. Hancock in his famous essay, *Australia*, argued:

> To the Australian, the State means collective power at the service of

---

108 J.A. La Nauze, *Alfred Deakin: A Biography*, Melbourne: Melbourne University Press, 1965, p.107.

individualistic 'rights'. Therefore he sees no opposition between his individualism and his reliance upon Government.[109]

Nor was Hancock's conclusion idiosyncratic. In fact the most famous forecast that democracy would give rise to expansive government had been made as far back as the 1830s by the French social scientist Alexis de Tocqueville (1835) as an outcome of his visit to America. In his view the constant attempts by individuals to secure their own purposes was an inexorable pressure on government that would inevitably lead to the regulation of all social life:

> Democratic ages are times of experiment, innovation and adventure. There are always a lot of men engaged in some difficult or new undertaking which they pursue apart, unencumbered by assistance. Such men will freely admit the general principle that the state should not interfere in private affairs, but as an exception, each one of them wants the state to help in the special matter with which he is preoccupied, and he wants to lead the government to take action in his domain, though he would like to restrict it in every other direction. As a multitude of people, all at the same moment, take this particular view about a great variety of different purposes, the sphere of central government insensibly expands in every direction, although every individual wants to restrict it...[110]

Tocqueville's well known forecast clearly identifies a mechanism by which an individualist culture can produce an expansive state: the unceasing pressures on government by private or special interests for laws and spending in their favour. Hancock's description of Australia is certainly compatible with Tocqueville's analysis. Nor, in the Australian case, does Hancock's conclusion by any means stand alone. One quite striking observation which supports it is that of the English Fabians, Sidney and Beatrice Webb, who visited Australia in 1898. The Webbs were hoping to find 'collectivism'. Instead, as Sidney Webb wrote to his friend Graham Wallas after the visit:

> ...you have here a genuine Democracy, the people really getting what it wishes to get... The trouble is that the people are an exceptionally

---

109 W.K. Hancock, *Australia*, Sydney: Jacaranda Press (1930), 1961, p.55.
110 Tocqueville, *Democracy in America*, p.648.

Individualist graft from our Individualist epoch (1840-1870)...[111]

From the 1830s observers of Australia had noted the dominance of the energetic pursuit of individual financial independence, and it is generally recognised by historians that it was this search that gave electoral force to the demand in the 1850s to open the inland plains to agricultural settlement. It was expressed in the development of the yeoman farming society of South Australia. Charles Darwin had noticed when he visited Sydney in the *Beagle* in 1836 that:

> The whole population, poor and rich, are bent on acquiring wealth; amongst the higher orders, wool and sheep grazing form the constant subject of conversation....[112]

The Webbs too had linked Australian individualism to 'new fabricated materialism'. Perhaps the most powerful evidence for this individualism can be seen in the early evolution of the tax system, and the reliance on debt financed development, emphasising the electoral resistance to government revenue raising. Most tax revenue was raised indirectly in Australia via revenue customs duties. Direct taxation was still a controversial notion as late as the decades 1890-1910 when the 'state experiments' of minimum wages and compulsory arbitration were first tried, and governments of all persuasions recognised that without debt financing the revenue could not be obtained to develop the continent at the speed international politics seemed to require. This large scale government spending was directed to providing public infrastructure to support private endeavour, and was thus fully compatible with an individualist culture.

In addition, however, to the pursuit of financial independence as a prominent cultural value, the development of the middle class in the second half of the nineteenth century was also accompanied by the strengthening influence in politics of humanitarian attitudes. Alfred Marshall had noted:

> A higher notion of social duty is spreading everywhere. In Parliament, in the press and in the pulpit, the spirit of humanity speaks more

---

111 Sidney and Beatrice Webb, *The Webbs' Australian Diary 1898*, A.G. Austin (ed.), Melbourne: Isaac Pitman and Sons, 1965, p.115.
112 Charles Darwin, *The Voyage of H.M.S. Beagle*, London: The Folio Society, 2003 (1839), p.442.

distinctly and more earnestly....[113]

As a cultural value of growing significance, humanitarianism was expressed through the evangelical churches in their missions to Aboriginal communities, and in the highly successful campaigns of the 1880s and 1890s against sweated labour. The political strength of humanitarianism was reinforced by the social research of Charles Booth into poverty in London and other British cities, and by the growing concern in North America with urban poverty alongside great wealth that had, inter alia, provided the title for Henry George's influential book *Progress and Poverty* (1879).[114]

Humanitarianism, like democracy itself, is an individualist idea. Democracy meant political equality for each person, not for classes, nor collectives. The unalienable 'rights' of each person to the liberty to pursue happiness specified by Jefferson were rights possessed by every individual person. Bellamy indeed had argued that it was necessary to truncate political rights to achieve the collective purposes of his utopia. Humanitarianism, deriving its definition and political force from Wilberforce's anti-slavery campaigns, based its value system around the common humanity of each person, and the policy solution to humanitarian problems was to elevate each individual, not a class. Paradoxically, where collectivism might sacrifice individual purposes in the pursuit of some 'common good', the idea of individualism supported solutions that helped all, on the basis that every individual was of equal worth and had equal rights.

What were the main components of the individualist culture? The defining element was the pursuit of purposes identified by individuals – whether selfish or altruistic – rather than purposes enforced by some external source – a church or religion, a paternalistic aristocracy, an ideological movement or an empire. Immigrants to Australia, it seems, broadly wanted to pursue their own purposes, rather than live their lives according to the dictates of a social class system, an established

---

113 Marshall, *Principles*, p.765.
114 Henry George, *Progress and Poverty: An Inquiry into the Cause of Industrial Depressions, and of Increase of Want with Increase of Wealth – the Remedy*, London: Kegan Paul, Trench & Co., 1879 [1884].

church, a social movement or a government. They had opportunities to do this in Australia they did not have in Britain. These purposes were generally seen as materialistic, though the extent of this 'materialism' has to be established. Financial independence is not necessarily sought for materialistic reasons, and indeed, may have benevolent purposes, or purposes related to any of the matters, including education and cultural endeavour or opportunities for one's children and family, for which money is relevant. What seems clear is that Australians generally sought financial wellbeing to pursue their purposes. We do know from the support for the churches that religious and often humanitarian objectives were prevalent in their considerations.

Once it is accepted that Australia's culture was, as observers noted, individualistic, its legitimacy in the eyes of the Australians, needs to be explained. The obvious source of this legitimacy is the liberal political culture of the leadership of government – pre- and post – the coming of democracy. From the 1830s, the elite political culture, indeed, began to take to itself the name 'Liberal'. The institutions and the politics within which the immigrants pursued their purposes were liberal, and there was a two-way interaction between the liberal ideas of the country's leaders and the individualism of the immigrants' purposes.

It is important to note that even as far back as the 1830s the leaders of political liberalism were not altogether at ease with the specific character of the cultural individualism that was developing in the Australian colonies. For people such as Governors Burke and Gipps, newspaper editors such as Hall, Duncan, and West, and later Liberals such as Griffith, Higinbotham, Wise, Pearson and Deakin, Australians were too selfish and sometimes too ruthless in their pursuit of private purposes, and their public spiritedness was too subdued, even for the comfortable operation of liberal institutions of government. The attacks on aboriginal people exemplified this, and showed the limited acceptance of the idea of a common humanity, and the obstacles to enforcing the rule of law. Liberals such as Griffith concluded, however, that these were problems of morality, rather than political philosophy, and could perhaps be solved, or at least mitigated, by the churches and by government action.

Pre-democratic liberalism and conservatism

Australia's political liberalism and individualist culture were clearly evident by the 1830s, though the main components of political liberalism had sailed with Arthur Phillip in the First Fleet. By 1788 the foundations of political economy, based on the idea of the spontaneous economic and social order that emerged with 'natural liberty', had been laid by Adam Smith; the techniques for securing legislative reform by policy analysis were already being developed by Jeremy Bentham; and William Wilberforce had already commenced his evangelical crusade against slavery and in favour of the common humanity of all mankind. Followers of Locke and Montesquieu had won the American Revolution and written the documents that embodied the ideal of 'unalienable' rights to life, liberty and the pursuit of happiness, to be secured by government with the consent of the people. A new concept of government in the public interest was emerging, and the possibility of engaging the mass of the people in the process of government was already being discussed. A year after Sydney Cove was occupied, the French Revolution broke out, attempting to secure American liberty for the European continent. Australia was founded in the age of liberalism, and its immigrant society, emancipist and free, embraced its ideas.

There followed some years in which conservative views of economic policy and government in the private interest of the aristocratic class did battle with those that supported economic liberty. The more liberal minded, pursuing their own individual purposes, used the new ideas to oppose the shipping monopoly of the East India company, lobby against British protection which discriminated against Australian products and the trading monopolies of the NSW Corps, and support broader participation in government. The 'rights' of Englishmen, trial by jury, freedom of the press and representative government were being demanded by the 1820s. Whigs such as William Charles Wentworth and Tories such as the Macarthurs (John and his sons) brought the policy stances and attitudes of English politics to the debate over Australian development.

The leader of political liberalism in Australia at the time, and the man who entrenched it in the Australian political culture as a viable philosophy of government, was the Governor from 1831-1837 Sir Richard Bourke, with the assistance of the man described by John Dunmore Lang as Bourke's Prime Minister, Francis Forbes, Chief Justice of the Supreme Court. Bourke was a Whig and a liberal Anglican with a strong belief in the need for reform, and his appointment had followed the coming to office of the Whigs at Westminster in November 1830. His Governorship brought to Australia a self-consciously liberal regime that set out to promote the norms of the rule of law, a liberal economy, social equality, freedom of the press, freedom of religion, universal education, protection of native peoples, and a moral law-abiding culture. In New South Wales, some of these were radical and even inflammatory notions among the conservatives. The more liberal character of the colonial Whigs was welcome to Bourke as he struggled with his Tory-dominated Executive Council.

It was during the 1830s that the term 'liberal' first came into common use as a political label both in Britain and Australia. John Dunmore Lang, in his inimitable style, characterised the two 'parties':

> The Liberals, as they have chosen to style themselves, comprehend in politics, Whigs, Reformers, Radicals, and Republicans, in all their motley varieties; and in religion, Papists, Dissenters, Deists, Atheists and Anythingarians.[115]

Lang chose to contrast his 'Liberals' with those he termed the 'Bigots', who were:

> in politics, Tories, Conservatives and Aristocrats, under various modifications; and in religion (so far, at least, as the British Empire is concerned) Christians, in contradistinction from infidels – Protestants, in contradistinction from Papists – and Established Churchmen, in contradistinction from Dissenters.[116]

Most observers gave 'liberalism' a more modest and moderate meaning than Lang. 'Liberalism' now was a term whose conventional connotation was well stated by the *Sydney Monitor* in December 1837 when it recorded the assessment in *Murray's Review* that the British Ministerial arrangements reported at the prorogation of parliament in

---

115 *The Colonist*, 23/2/37, p.1.
116 *The Colonist*, 23/2/37, p.1.

July "give promise of Liberalism", to the extent of "Whig and something more".[117]

A feature of this early period, nevertheless, is that it was almost the last moment in Australian history, until the 1990s, when a political conservatism existed that accepted the label, and that conservatism was already by the 1830s incorporating the liberal spirit of the age. In the 1830s there were Australian political activists ready to accept the label 'Tory'. They were already, however, prime examples of a 'rugged' individualism.

The rise to intellectual dominance of liberal ideas at the time, and the rapid establishment in Australia of an officially sanctioned culture of individual freedom, meant that expressions of conservative views were invariably accompanied by liberal rhetoric. This is illustrated in James Macarthur's contribution to the 1833 Court House debate on a Petition for a House of Assembly:

> As a native of this Colony, a name of which I am proud (hear, hear), and as one having a considerable stake in the Colony, I must say it is painful to me to be taunted as an enemy to Liberty. Gentlemen, I am no enemy to Liberty! (Hear, hear) I am as great an advocate for the enjoyment of our rights, as any gentleman in this Colony! (Cheers). I did not come here today to oppose Liberty. I came here to support it! But, gentlemen, I wished to support freedom in a way that I considered calculated to ensure our success.[118]

These landowners both regarded themselves, and were regarded by others, as the Australian expression of the 'aristocratic' interest that was still then dominant in British politics. They saw the wool industry they were building as the main development prospect for Australia, and believed that on their success depended the very viability of the Australian settlement. Economically, given the high cost of attracting labourers to the distant runs, they wanted cheap convict labour, or alternatively a free labour market that allowed them to bring labourers from India and China.

Their conservatism was expressed in a cautious attitude to political reform, and in particular, to the extension of the electorate, which

---

117 *Sydney Monitor*, 6/12/37.
118 *Sydney Monitor*, 2/2/1833, p.3.

they feared would undermine the availability of the low cost labour provided by the convict system. In their efforts to build a true colonial aristocracy they had an explicit concern with civility in politics and with a belief in organised religion as the source of the moral basis for civil order. Conservatives supported strong governmental authority to suppress crime and outbreaks of political violence (if any), and feared liberals would be weaker against criminals. They preferred Tory to Whig-appointed Governors. As in England, liberty and licence were often linked by conservatives, and this became the main theme of their representations to the Molesworth Committee of the House of Commons in 1837 over the issue of transportation and its link to the form of the colonial constitution.

The main activist opponent of the colonial Tories, William Charles Wentworth, regarded himself as a Whig, and remained such throughout his life, a strong supporter of the liberal principles of the Glorious Revolution of 1688 and the Bill of Rights of 1689 which emphasised parliamentary control over taxation and spending, to which he added, the liberalism of the equality of emancipists and free emigrants, free trade and individual enterprise, the separation of church and state and the enlightenment role of reason in public affairs. He remained an opponent of universal suffrage throughout almost his whole political career. As a more democratic liberalism emerged, Wentworth was increasingly regarded as a conservative, but his was rather a conservative liberalism, which he embodied in the 1855 NSW Constitution (for the drafting of which he was mainly responsible).

When one looks closely at the political debates over representation in colonial government during the 1830s, it becomes evident that the strength of the idea of individual freedom in Australia was great. Free emigrants, ex-convicts, pastoralists and farmers, importers and shopkeepers, all supported it. The colonial Tories wanted the political and economic freedom to achieve their agenda, while the emigrants who had recently arrived after experiencing the agitation over the 1832 Reform Act, and who had been trained in the political associations which had achieved it, wanted even greater freedom to pursue their financial independence and wider representation so their voice would be heard politically. The concept of a civil freedom accepted by the leading liberals in the colony such as Edward Smith Hall, the editor of the *Sydney Monitor*, was expansive:

> By freedom we mean freedom to do good, coupled with restraint to do harm. By freedom we mean liberty to do to others, as we should wish, were we in their circumstances to be done unto; freedom to do by ourselves and for ourselves, everything that is good and pleasant *that will not injure others*; but to be restrained, whenever we wish to gratify ourselves at the expense of others' comfort or well-being. This is what we call *civil and religious freedom*...[119]

Hall himself had accepted imprisonment from the Tory Governor Sir Richard Darling in defence of freedom of the press.

Hall had commented ironically, doubtless with James Macarthur's liberal rhetoric in mind:

> It is the fashion now-a-days for Ultra Tories to express the most enthusiastic admiration of civil and religious freedom; but it is of freedom at a *distance*; freedom *another* time; freedom in the abstract; not tangible freedom, now and here.[120]

Colonial Tories and Whigs both insisted on a property qualification for the vote. The more radical liberals were prepared to open the voting right to those with "qualifications of the mind", to use the phrase of William Bland, an educated emancipist.[121]

Australian conservatism was transformed during the 1840s by the onset of the squatting age. The emancipist/emigrant argument dissipated as propertied Whigs and Tories joined political forces to secure title to the vast landed estates they were occupying on the inland plains, against the resistance of Governor Sir George Gipps, Bourke's liberal successor.

It was as much as anything else the sheer scale of the Australian continent that was to make it obvious to the British government that the future of New South Wales was as a free colony based on private enterprise and private investment. As the government struggled to keep up with the spontaneous expansion, and available public capital fell far

---

119 *Sydney Monitor*, 16/3/1833, p.3.
120 *Sydney Monitor*, 10/4/1833, p.2.
121 *Sydney Monitor*, 2/2/1/33, p.3.

short of requirements, the 1830s became the high water-mark of private leadership in Australia's economic growth. "In the 1830s the NSW economy was perhaps more fully private than it had ever been before and was ever to be thereafter."[122]

Liberal Democracy

By 1850, therefore, Australia was already developing a highly individualist culture, justified, explained and endorsed by a political elite imbued with liberal ideas, and increasingly calling itself Liberal. This individualism grasped the idea of democracy with enthusiasm, and the new democratic states would be seized upon as ideal instruments to open opportunities for all, and provide the infrastructure to support private endeavour. The Liberal Catholicism of leaders such as O'Shanassy and Gavan Duffy sat alongside the radical Liberal Protestantism of George Higinbotham in Victoria and Charles Lilley in Queensland. It was a potent mix with an inevitable outcome. Liberal democrats such as Charles Cowper, Henry Parkes, Richard Dry, John West, William Westgarth, and others seized the initiative through the Anti-Transportation League to force the capitulation of the British government on transportation policy, and to achieve self-government. The leaders of the League became the political leaders of new Australian democracies and by the end of the 1850s had defeated those who wished to import not only the British reformed Whig constitution but a British style aristocracy as well.

Australian political conservatism, with its focus on private enterprise-based economic development, would evolve in its policy philosophy towards an emphasis on economic freedom and support for an absolute personal liberty as advocated by Herbert Spencer in *Social Statics* (1850).[123] The conservative attitude translated into economic policy would thus evolve towards the most extreme and even utopian version of liberalism, *laissez faire* libertarianism. Private enterprise and the market freedom believed to be inherent in the ownership of property would be given its full scope in their thinking. But it was not greatly different in this

---

122 N.G. Butlin, *Forming a Colonial Economy: Australia 1810-1850*, Cambridge: Cambridge University Press, 1994, p.121.
123 Herbert Spencer, *Social Statics*, NY, D. Appleton & Co., (1850) 1892.

regard to the classical liberalism of the British Liberal Party. It seemed conservative rather than radical in the Australian environment because it was challenged in the political sphere by the agendas of the new Liberal parties for increased state action in the pursuit of further democratic and later humanitarian goals.

Individualism, Collectivism and State Experiments

Liberal parties as parliamentary and even electoral organisations began to evolve as soon as democracy was established in the late 1850s. Charles Lilley established a Liberal Party in Queensland in 1859, and from that emerged the well organised and popularly structured Liberal Party of Samuel Griffith twenty years later. In Victoria parliamentary Liberal groupings can be identified from the 1850s, and in 1879 Graham Berry, supported by Charles Pearson and others, brought the Land and Protection Leagues together in a rejuvenated Liberal Party drawing strong support from an emerging working class and trade union movement. In New South Wales, where Parkes' free trade party was dominant, a free trade Liberal Party to oppose the protectionism seeping in from Victoria was established in 1889, though Parkes made clear that he regarded his own earlier political associations as also being Liberal.

These Liberal parties all opposed squatter dominance, supported the opening of the lands to agricultural settlement, and in the mines and cities supported factory legislation and the legalisation of trade union activity. They established universal secular public education with equal primary education for boys and girls. Their philosophical and policy guide was John Stuart Mill, but all of them were under pressure from Mill's *bete noir*, the Christian churches, for legislation to enforce religious observance and public morality. The dominance of the policy thinking of Mill expressed in his *Principles of Political Economy* (1848)[124] had one great exception: the Victorian Liberal Party, under relentless pressure on public opinion and governments from the anti-English Scot, David Syme, the proprietor of *The Age*, had become protectionist, a decision which was to make it the creator of a new and powerful political vested

---

124 John Stuart Mill, *Principles of Political Economy*, London, Longmans, Green and Co., 1902 [1848].

interest: a government-dependent manufacturing sector.

Nothing showed the dominance of the Liberal movement in Australia by 1890 more than the composition of the Convention called to draft a Constitution for a nation embracing all the colonies. The delegates were spread across the Liberal spectrum. They labelled each other variously as 'conservatives', 'radicals', 'extreme democrats' and even 'reactionaries', according to the stances they perceived each adopted towards existing interests and institutions, but all assumed the validity of the liberal project whose principles of government they sought to embody in the Constitution.

In a letter to Charles Henry Pearson, Deakin, with his great interest in political labels, said that Downer was 'the Conservative spokesman except in Judicial matters", that the Western Australians were "solidly and stolidly" Conservative, and that this was true also of his colleague Gillies, except on the issue of Senate powers. Nevertheless his principal allies were Gillies, Parkes, and Playford, with support from Barton, Griffith & Clark.[125] It was a glittering concourse of talent, and the quality of the debates was widely regarded as worthy of the objective of creating a new nation of free people.

The Constitution, however, had been drawn up in the evening of the Liberal consensus in Australia. By 1890 that consensus was already under extreme pressure, as Liberals debated amongst each other over the role of the state in promoting the development of an Australian nation and realising the full promise of democracy. The threads in the liberal intellectual tradition which had led inexorably to conflict over the role (and scope) of government were several, as each played out its own internal logic. It was on the basis of this individualist culture and a humanitarian political liberalism that the explosion of the size of government in Australia occurred.

Free Trade, Protection and Conservatism

The free trade/protection dispute that engaged Australia's political/policy leaders for several decades at the end of the nineteenth and early twentieth centuries became a classic example of a public policy debate

---

125 La Nauze, *Alfred Deakin*, p.48.

arising from special interest claims for privileges from the state, and hence an influential pressure for the growth of government. Its full significance for the future cannot be understood without recognising that it was also a debate carried on at the intellectual level among policy analysts outside Australia, and that one of the reasons why Australia plunged into protectionism, as had America, was the absence from Australia of any level of sophisticated policy analysis.

All the leading political economists since Adam Smith – Ricardo, McCulloch, Mill, and Marshall, and many others – recommended free trade as the basic policy to stimulate economic growth, though Mill had left the door open to short-term and temporary protection of domestic industry in new nations, where there was a prospect of establishing a new industry that could be internationally competitive because of natural advantages. It was a narrow crack, but through it the Victorian Liberals had been pushed by Syme into a protectionist/nationalist position which ultimately rejected the mainstream of economic theory. Tariff protection for Australian manufacturing was an extension of government action opposed by importing mercantile interests and by the pastoralists, and by those knowledgeable in political economy, but it was capable of being sold as a populist nationalist and democratic policy, and was so sold.

At its core the debate was between the advocates of a concept of an Australia that was open to the world, innovative and competitive, and an Australia increasingly closed in upon itself, driven by the belief that it could use government to secure a standard of living in Australia higher than in the rest of the (English-speaking) world. The hope was vain, because the instrument (protection) would not achieve the efficient competitive domestic industries its proponents claimed, and the door to the outside world was not entirely closed, and the whole experiment was irretrievably vulnerable to international market forces which were beyond the control of Australian governments, or industries. As costs rose, exports of Australian manufactures declined, and the whole redistributive arrangement of new protection (through the arbitration system) depended on commodity prices. When they declined, the system stumbled.

In 1903 Reid, leader of the free trade Liberals, crystallised the issues when he appealed to the Liberal protectionists:

> I ask you not to assist to shatter the rapidly growing trade of Australia with the rest of the world. Is it not a mad thing to drive people away, and madder to shut ports against customers? Is this not the latest phase of protectionist lunacy? The protectionists in Victoria swore for protection for that State, and yet they shouted for the free trade [with the other colonies] that federation brought.... [T]he protectionists [are] afraid of the oceans: of all the facilities which the Creator and the inventive genius of man had supplied to bring the nations of the world together. The fight for protection [is] a fight against the progress of the world.[126]

Reid himself, who had been a great reforming Premier in New South Wales, noted in 1901 that "It had been said that the free traders of Victoria were conservative, that they were afraid of political progress".

> I will tell you that the Free Trade Party is not a conservative party. We are not fearful of political progress. The grand old chiefs of liberal reform in the mother state [NSW] were all free trade champions. They were not liberals because they were free traders. Being liberals, they could not help being free traders. Let it not be forgotten that outside Victoria the great bulk of the masses of the people are free traders.[127]

Reid accurately predicted that the inevitable result of adopting the policy of protecting uncompetitive industries would be to fill the lobbies of parliament with businesses seeking state support. The special interests that were created by the policy of protection indeed soon became too powerful to permit its abolition, regardless of what economists such as Alfred Marshall, Mill's successor as the leading world economist, and a strong supporter of free trade, might say. These interests included the Labor Party from 1910 onwards. By 1909, indeed, it was to be the Victorian protected manufacturers who would take the initiative in establishing Deakin's Commonwealth Liberal Party. A policy once regarded as 'radical' had established a powerful conservative interest.

From the perspective of the twenty-first century Reid can be seen

---

126 *Sydney Morning Herald*, 16/11/03, p.7.
127 *The Argus*, 13/8/1901, p.5.

as the authentic voice of a progressive liberalism, yet at the time Alfred Deakin described his free-trading opponents as 'conservatives', on the ground that they represented the 'vested interests' of the importers and were sceptical of the reforms he was promoting – compulsory arbitration and his new system of redistribution to wages called 'new protection'. By contrast the manufacturers who had emerged in Victoria under the policy of protection, and backed him, called themselves 'Liberals'. Ironically, the policy of protection at the time was the policy of the British Conservative Party, while the British Liberal Party was still resolutely a free trade party. Deakin's labelling of the free traders illustrates how time- and context-specific are political labels, but particularly the label 'conservative'. Deakin's so-called 'conservatives' were by then, the main defenders of the market economy, and regarded themselves as the true 'Liberals'.

When the free trade Liberals (based in New South Wales) and the protectionist Liberals (based in Victoria) came together in the first united federal Liberal party in 1909 Reid declared:

> Indeed, I believe it is a mere political trick of the most obvious kind to endeavour to describe any party, either in the Federal or the State arena, as a Conservative Party. There is no such party in Australia. There is no country in the world where the people are less paralysed by a reverence for the past....[128]

The true political battle in Australia, Reid had argued since 1905, was between those who believed in the liberal economy based on private enterprise and those who would extend the sphere of government to interfere with and replace the market. Reid believed that within Labor's platform, and especially among the more ideological of its trade union adherents, the seeds had already been planted for the destruction of the liberal political, social and economic system to which he had committed his life. In his view, the Labor Party, in which a collectivist ideology was increasingly influential, was a "dangerous enemy", and unity among the Liberals would be essential to safeguard the liberal system.[129] Reid

---

128 Rod Kemp and Marion Stanton (eds.), *Speaking for Australia: Parliamentary speeches that shaped our nation,* Sydney: Allen & Unwin, 2004, p.37.
129 Sir George Reid, *My Reminiscences,* London: Cassell & Co., 1917, p.245.

thus identified the political parties as key mechanisms for controlling the growth of government, and the development of this issue over the coming decades would illustrate the soundness of his analysis.

Laissez-Faire versus Intervention
The free trade/protection debate overlaid another fundamental debate within liberalism. On one side of this debate was the *laissez-faire* or, perhaps more correctly, libertarian liberalism of the kind advocated by Herbert Spencer and represented politically, to a large extent, by W.E. Gladstone in Britain and by Liberals such as Henry Parkes, Bruce Smith and William McMillan in Australia. On the other side was the socially interventionist 'new' liberalism of a Chamberlain, or in Australia a Berry, a Pearson or a Deakin.

While the two sides of the debate over 'new' liberalism are sometimes aligned with the free trade/protection debate (and in Chamberlain they came to be so aligned), in Australia these were overlapping but distinct debates. Some of the strongest advocates of free trade – such as George Reid and Bernhard Wise – were comfortable with state regulation of industry for humanitarian purposes, as were the English economists Toynbee and Marshall and their followers, and it was this fact – and the willingness of both Reid and Wise to ally themselves with Labor early on in the pursuit of humane economic regulation (though Wise went much further than Reid) that had ensured the political defeat of Spencer's (and Bruce Smith's) libertarian liberalism in Australia by the end of the nineteenth century.

Spencer's libertarianism by the late nineteenth century, however, had become the dominant ideology in private enterprise, and it can be considered as the most thorough-going ideological and policy expression of the broader individualism in the culture. Its defeat came about because of the emergence in Australia of a political alliance between the humanitarian attitudes of Australia's large and influential middle class, and the world's most powerful trade union movement, both products of Australia's individualist and democratic culture.

The strength of Australian unionism was to a significant extent the result of liberal policies and the all-pervading democratic ethos of the colonies. In Australia as in Britain the liberals had taken the lead in removing from trade unions the legal restrictions that had been imposed on them by the dominant employers of the pre-Reform Act era. Universal education, a mobile immigrant society, and an egalitarian, democratic and humanitarian culture, provided fertile ground for the idea that employees should have rights to influence the management of the firm, and thus for the growth of unionism.

There is wide agreement amongst historians that the surge in union membership in Australia in the late 1880s was not the result of exploitation, but rather of a growing belief in the capacity of organised workers in Australia to alter workplace relations without the intervention of the state. The eight-hour day had been achieved in this way. By 1890 some 20 per cent of the workforce was unionised, compared with perhaps 5 per cent in the United States.

The strength of the union movement was welcomed by the liberals, many of whom wanted to assist it to expand further. Liberals drew strong electoral support from trade unionists and the broader working class, and in 1889 the president of the Melbourne Trades Hall Council, William Trenwith, was elected a Liberal Party Member of Parliament. What became significant for union and Liberal attitudes to the role of government, particularly, was the hold gained within the Australian union movement, together with its influence on Liberals in both Australia and New Zealand, of the utopian socialism of Edward Bellamy's *Looking Backward* (overlaid on Henry George's support for land nationalisation).

Many of the ideas in Bellamy's book: the possibility of the abolition of strikes, of a peaceful 'transition to socialism' with middle class support, the efficiency of centralisation in industry and government, the end of competition and the nationalisation of industries, were to echo in labour thought and political programs for decades. Marxist, Fabian and other socialist ideas were used to persuade many workers that solutions to social problems through government were not only practicable, but even 'scientific'. If ever there was a moment when a genuine collectivism might have established itself in Australian culture this was it, but in fact it never achieved wide support outside the union elites, the new Labour Party, and a segment of the Liberals. Its popular expression, encouraged by these elites, indeed soon came to be a culture among union members of class war and a belief in an expansive role for the state to control industry and redistribute wealth.

It is significant in understanding the links between culture, political ideas, and policy outcomes that the growing popularity of socialist ideas did not at first point Australian unionism towards the state as the solution to labour problems. By 1890 Australian unionism led by W.G. Spence had come to the conclusion that it was strong enough to achieve, outside the state, a 'reconstruction of society' that would redefine the 'rights' of private property in industry, and force employers in the major industrial workplaces – in wool, coal mining, rail, waterfront and shipping – to manage in future under union contracts, and to employ only unionists. Spence described himself as a socialist, and his attempts to redefine the scope of management authority inherent in private property, mark him out as well outside the liberal mainstream. Even he conceded the 'co-operative' society was for the future, but though not an immediate goal, was an inspiration. His motivation was rather more democratic (i.e. union) control of the workplace. It was the disastrous failure of this bold attempt that led the unions to turn to government action to improve the conditions and wages of workers and, in the short term, to adopt more limited (and more individualist) Liberal reform programs, which the various supporters of collectivism worked hard to radicalise.

We can mark the failure of the strikes of 1890-1891 as the moment when significant elements within Australian liberalism at a political level lost sight of the essential significance of market competition in the functioning of the liberal economy, and it was the for the most part, though not entirely, the protectionists, who had already ignored this in relation to international trade, who led the way. The protectionist Liberals began occasionally to use the word 'socialist' to describe themselves, including people such as Deakin and Eggleston. None of them were committed followers of Bellamy, though most, at least, had read him, and perhaps had taken inspiration from him. The chief liberal initiator of the state experiments that followed, the New Zealander William Pember Reeves, the author of the first compulsory arbitration act, though calling himself a liberal, was a self-confessed policy 'socialist' who had declared:

> There were many degrees of Socialism just as there were in Liberalism....In a democratic country the State could do for the people as a whole a great deal of good. It could break up the land monopoly, regulate the employment of labour, and find employment for those who want it. There were many things which the State could do to ameliorate the condition of the people that could not be done by the people themselves individually. He was one of those Socialists who believed that the functions of the state should be extended as much as possible, and not restricted.[130]

In response to the failure of the union campaign to rein in the employers, sympathetic liberals began to legislate for limitations on the hours of work, minimum wages and ultimately, and most significantly, compulsory arbitration to end industrial disputes once and for all. In New South Wales Bernhard Wise, a free trader, who would follow Reeves in legislating compulsory arbitration in that state in 1901, declared in 1891 that all men should join unions and that the need was to lift the working class as a whole. The emergence of a small Labor party holding the balance of power meant that, despite the passionate resistance of the market Liberals, Spencerian and otherwise, the anti-competition 'reformers' were able to achieve significant success.

Compulsory arbitration was a profoundly anti-individualist and in many ways illiberal piece of legislation. To a significant degree it rejected the market determination of wages and conditions of work, and was a severe qualification to the competitive labour market. It was designed deliberately to change the balance of power between employers and employees, or unionists, but it favoured unions and, at the same time, deprived individuals of their right to representation, and qualified through union preference the right of individuals to employment. It imposed decisions on employers who had not been represented before the arbitration court. It sought to force individual workers into unions. As Reeves had made clear: "The Act conferred no status on a workman

---

130 *Thames Star*, 9/4/1895, p.4.

who was not a member of a union... The non-unionist had no legal right to demand employment."[131] George Reid described Wise's principle of the common rule, which permitted the Court to direct and bind people who had not appeared before it, as "a more monstrous and infamous perversion of every principle of British justice than had ever been proposed in any Parliament in the world".[132]

The motivations were humanitarian, but utopian, and to achieve these ends established liberal economic and legal principles were sacrificed. Alfred Deakin, in supporting compulsory arbitration of industrial disputes, famously thought that it would achieve Bellamy's objective of abolishing strikes. He declared:

> This Bill marks, in my opinion, the beginning of a new phase of civilization. It begins the establishment of the People's Peace....It is not a matter of today or tomorrow.... It is the introduction of a new principle, which, when it has found its proper means of exerting its influence, will comprehend necessarily as great a transformation in the features of industrial society as the creation of the Kings Peace brought about in Civil society.[133]

The utopian spirit had thus gripped some of the most influential leaders of Australian liberalism. If Spencer's libertarianism, as expressed by Bruce Smith, had become utopian, so had liberal protectionism. What would be the actual effects of the Australasian 'state experiments' by the 'new' liberals was unclear in the absence of any sophisticated policy analysis. Marshall, at Cambridge, commented meaningfully on "rapid advances on untried paths, for the safety of which the only guarantees offered were the confident hopes of men whose imaginations were eager, but not steadied by knowledge nor by the discipline of hard thought."[134] He was determined to keep such 'state experiments' out of Britain.

Labor's utopianism at the parliamentary level extended considerably further than that of the liberals. Nationalisation of key industries, the efficiency of centralisation, the end of competition, and the possibility

---

131 William Pember Reeves, *State Experiments in Australia and New Zealand*, Vols. I & II, London: George Allen & Unwin Ltd., 1902, p.122.
132 *Sydney Morning Herald*, 18/9/1900, p.3.
133 Commonwealth Parliamentary Debates, HoR, 30 July 1904, p.2864.
134 Marshall, *Principles*, I, pp.47-48.

of a transition to socialism (by class war if necessary) held a grip on the party's imagination for decades. Nevertheless, Labor's liberal socialist leaders Watson, Fisher and Hughes were as sceptical as the liberals of the possibility of Australia's individualist culture being replaced by a society based on compulsory 'co-operation', and each of them rejected the collectivist utopianism of many of their colleagues. The party's programs before World War I were largely drawn from the liberals, and though leaders such as Fisher were more comfortable with the term 'socialism' to describe policies of selective nationalisation and intervention, liberals such as Wise, Deakin, and Eggleston were not too uncomfortable with admitting that they were themselves partly socialist. Being socialist did not mean acceptance of class war attitudes. It meant to them simply a positive attitude towards the role of government in solving humanitarian problems.

Indeed, the 'socialism' that led liberals such as Irvine, Bent and Eggleston to experiment with government-owned enterprises to manage railways, electricity, roads and water generation, while idealistic to the point of utopianism in their belief in the willingness of independent men to work for the public interest, was driven by their wish to avoid the political corruption that accompanied the conduct of such services by commissioners subject to parliamentary interference. Paradoxically, it was their ethical desire to avoid the temptations of political control over expanding government services that led them to further 'state experiments', designed to be actually independent of democratic control, which in their eyes could be too easily led astray. They hoped that the mechanism of the independent statutory authority would protect the expanding government from the pressure of private interests to divert the state to their own benefit.

Thus, as compulsory arbitration was being legislated, liberalism at the state level led by Irvine in Victoria was busy establishing a range of statutory authorities, notionally 'independent' of politics, to provide services in areas such as railways and trams, electricity and gas, water and urban planning, and country roads. Those who theorised on these matters assumed that the managers and the customers of these authorities would recognise that they were there to serve the public interest, and that they would evoke the sense of community co-operation that Pearson had believed would develop under democracy. Frederic Eggleston in 1930 claimed that "in proportion to the size and economic standing of the community [the Victorian State utilities] constitute possibly the largest and most comprehensive use of State power outside Soviet Russia."[135]

Labor Individualism

Despite the existence of government initiatives that in some respects reflected the adoption by Australian liberal leaders of collectivist values, at the political leadership levels individualist values and their traditional liberal justifications remained dominant. This is strikingly to be seen in a series of articles by, arguably, the most influential Labor leader in Australia, W.M. Hughes. In his *Case for Labour* (1910), Hughes explicitly rejected the anti-individualist versions of socialism. He condemned those for whom the "ideal State is one in which the sphere within which individuals are free to act is reduced to a minimum".

> This I conceive to be a grand error, responsible for much of the opposition to collectivism. For the ideal State is surely one in which State Acts are reduced to a minimum and individuals permitted the widest possible freedom. For no man loves compulsion, but at best endures it. And it is for liberty, increased opportunities for self development and for happiness, that many, from whom come these demands for restrictive legislation, cry out.[136]

Properly conceived, Hughes argued, certain kinds of collectivism and liberty were compatible. Some restrictive legislation had actually increased liberty, he argued, but this did not mean that all restrictive legislation would do so. The basic principle justifying state interference with the individual was a similar principle to that which Mill had enunciated and that the liberals agreed with:

> The fundamental and primary principle underlying the relationship between the State and the individual, is that the former is justified in interfering with the individual's freedom of action when, and only when, this freedom is incompatible with that of other individuals.[137]

---

135 F.W. Eggleston, *State Socialism in Victoria*, London: P.S. King & Son, 1932, p.1.
136 William Morris Hughes, *The Case for Labor*, Sydney: Sydney University Press, 1970 [1910].
137 Ibid, 64.

Hughes moreover accepted that it was a fundamental principle of liberty that the individual should be allowed to be happy "in his own way". The state should leave that to the judgement of the individual. Of course, "to help him judge rightly, the State should rightly educate him. If his happiness can be secured more effectively and more easily in any other way, then that way will and ought to be preferred to collectivism"[138]. The mistake of many of those who called themselves liberals, Hughes argued, was that they refused to apply Mill's 'harm' principle in the industrial sphere.[139]

While Deakin and his followers, despite their liberal socialism, continued to see private enterprise and the decentralisation of the power of government through federalism as two of the essential foundations of liberalism, Hughes was much more willing to regulate and nationalise private industry, and was a firm believer in the centralisation and even unification of governmental power. Later Hughes, the war-time leader, was to become the ultra-protectionist, the founder of government-owned shipping and of government marketing and licensing of the production of rural industries, and the defender of compulsory arbitration, when most of the remaining liberals had recognised that, despite Deakin's initial utopian hopes, it was never going to be the road to industrial peace and harmony. What seems apparent is that during this period of Australian history the liberalism of the nation's political leaders did not give weight to, or even comprehend, the significance of competitive markets in products and labour for efficiency and productivity.

The parochial nationalism that had been fostered by protection, white Australia, and the Australian monopolies in coastal shipping and other regulations, encouraged a cultural attitude that the external world was to be feared, and that Australians could not compete. Political leaders asserted continually that it was possible for a nation protected from international competition to have efficient low cost industries, and that the use of the judiciary to determine 'fair' wages and conditions of work, would not only be acceptable to unionised workers, but, even if it made some businesses uneconomic, would not undermine employment

---

138 Ibid, 64.
139 Ibid, 60.

or prosperity, or inhibit capital investment.

The idea that an Australian standard of living above that of other countries could be maintained in such a closed economy depended ultimately on the redistribution of the profits of the world competitive industries, wool and wheat, and especially wool. If these ceased to flow, the whole utopian dream would collapse. The idea that the state encouragement of union membership under the compulsory arbitration system might create a powerful conservative labour interest, and might indeed provide an incentive for capture by extremists, was little considered.

Liberals Retreat from Utopia

Yet it was not long before the first signs of a retreat by the Liberals who had flirted with utopianism were apparent, and the first faltering steps towards this retreat can be read in the journal of Deakin's People's Liberal Party in Victoria, *The Liberal* (1911).

The Liberal had no doubt that the essence of liberalism was its support for the right of people to live their own lives, exercise freedom of speech and association, and to do political battle against the 'social tyranny' of corporatist unionism and utopian socialism, and against government that interfered excessively with private enterprise. Deakin's party journal, edited by his son-in-law Herbert Brookes, declared:

> To a Liberal the chief end of Government is liberty for each and all its citizens. Liberalism makes men most completely master of their own faculties, and opens to them the largest sphere of independent action. Co-operation in all its forms is fostered under Liberalism when consistent with the individual liberty essential to the manhood and womanhood of a free people.[140]

As the anti-capitalist class warriors gained increasing power within Labor before World War I, Deakin more and more came to emphasise the support of liberalism for private enterprise, though the government service monopolies were generally free of his criticism. That was to come later, as Eggleston's doubts grew to a certainty. These early doubts, however, were not to be expressed in policy retreat, because the First

---

140 *The Liberal*, vol.1, no.1, p.1.

World War was to further amplify and exaggerate the policy tendencies of the pre-war years.

The 1914-1918 war led to a vast expansion in the role of government in the economy, setting precedents for the most detailed regulation of rural industries, especially in relation to the pooling and marketing of commodities. Under criticism from the Liberal Party Hughes established a Commonwealth Shipping Line to facilitate exports. The Liberals argued a competitive tender would have been more sensible and economical. Existing taxes were increased and new taxes imposed.

Succession duties were introduced in 1914, a Commonwealth income tax was imposed for the first time in 1915. In 1917 a war-time profits tax was introduced, the land tax rates were increased, an entertainment indirect tax was levied from 1917, and tariff rates were scaled up, not just for protection but to raise revenue. By 1917-18 income tax was raising £7.4 million, while customs and excise raised £13.2 million. The latter was actually a declining source of revenue, however, as imports fell as a result of the war. As the States were already levying all these taxes (except the war-time profits tax) the Commonwealth entry into the field meant that the problem of double-taxation became a real one.[141] By the end of the war, taxation as a percentage of GDP had risen to over 9 per cent – an increase of 50 per cent over pre-war levels[142] – though way below what was required to finance the war, or to pay for developments.

The war heightened anti-capitalist radicalism within the union movement, and the leaders of the utopian push seized control of the Labor Party, transforming it unmistakably into a movement dominated by its extra-parliamentary forces. One by one the liberal socialist leaders were alienated. Fisher retired sick. Hughes and many of his Ministry were expelled, and the world's first Labor prime minister, Watson, joined them and left the Labor Party.

The devastating human disaster of the war submerged liberalism in

---

141 D.B. Copland, 'Australia in the World War, Economic', in J.H. Rose, A.P. Newton, and E.A. Benians, *The Cambridge History of the British Empire*, Cambridge: Cambridge University press, 1933, pp.587-604.
142 Vamplew, *Australians: Historical Statistics*, p.257.

Australia and was to destroy the Liberal Party in Britain. When in 1917 the Liberal Party absorbed Hughes' breakaway National Labor Party to form the 'win-the-war' Nationalist Party, it was generally seen to be a move towards a more radical, rather than a more conservative alliance, though its effect was conservative – to entrench the policy framework built around white Australia, compulsory arbitration, and tariff protection, a framework now locked in place politically by the Labor Party's willingness to campaign against any suggestion of policy retreat. It did not lead to a change in national policy directions, but pushed policy even more strongly towards economically non-competitive illiberal settings. The fusion of the Liberal Party with Hughes' National Labor party to become the Nationalists also meant that there was no organised voice to defend the Liberal tradition in Australia for almost three decades.

Reversing Mistakes

At the political level, the circumstances of the immediate post-war years led to a tangled confusion of political labels. This was not only because of the emergence of the Nationalist party, but was particularly because of the rise to political influence of explicit antagonists to liberalism in utopian communism and fascism. The 'social tyranny' feared by the Deakinite Liberals before the war had become stronger and more organised. The main concerns of Liberals (both protectionist and free trade) at the time were national development in the face of the anti-competitive policy framework, and the defence of liberal institutions against rampant anti-capitalism, expressed in utopian socialist terms. The Nationalist party brought together under the same roof conservatives, liberals, and former Labor liberal socialists. The scales of utopianism were falling from Liberal eyes, but the disentangling of a coherent thread of liberalism once more was to be the work of a political generation.

While organised liberalism was being destroyed in both Britain and Australia, politics in the two countries were in important respects 'out of sync'. In England the economist John Maynard Keynes was writing about the *End of Laissez-Faire* (1926), but in Australia, Frederic Eggleston pointed out, *laissez-faire* had ended a long time ago, and the Australians were wondering how to control the state. By the nineteen thirties the Australians had experimented with state action on a massive scale, and certainly some of the most thoughtful amongst them were dissatisfied with its results.

> Thus it is that while State action is looked on with favour by all the advanced parties in Great Britain to secure their aims, most thinking people in Australia are convinced that the inefficiencies of State action are responsible for many of our acute problems, and are looking for ways of limiting it.[143]

Those who had become active in the Liberal Party before the war, who supported protection, could see that Deakin's support for private enterprise and the decentralised federal constitution was under assault, that protection was beginning to blow out to extreme levels and that, in the context of a union movement under increasing influence from militants, the arbitration system had failed to secure Deakin's era of industrial peace. Neither Hughes nor Bruce were seen by such Liberals as suitable leaders. Hughes had declared in 1921 that:

> I have never been a supporter of the capitalistic system. I do not believe in it. But it is here. I see clearly its defects and obvious imperfections....It is a system which glorifies Mammon, but it is a system, modified by the great mass of the people coming into their heritage and using their power through the franchise to bend it to their ends, which is admirably adapted to the purposes of humanity.[144]

Hughes' declaration confronted the Liberals in the Nationalist alliance with a challenge. His attitude alienated many of the former Liberals, and marked him as an impossible leader for a party now under assault from a Labor Party in the grip of utopian socialism with an explicit socialist objective and alongside it an organised Communist Party. A debate began which continued throughout the 1920s among those who considered themselves spiritual Liberals over whether the Nationalist Party could be liberalised from within, or whether a new Liberal Party should be formed to challenge it from without.

---

143 Eggleston, *State Socialism in Victoria*, p.11.
144 L.F. Fitzhardinge, *William Morris Hughes: A Political Biography*, Vol II, Sydney: Angus & Robertson, 1979, p.507.

In 1921 a new party, the Liberal Union, was formed, declaring that the Nationalist Ministry had "no principles, neither those of Liberalism nor Socialism", and was "inefficient, extravagant, and politically demoralizing to a degree never before experienced in Australia."[145] It characterized the Nationalists as a wartime coalition that had outlived its purpose. The Liberal Union's candidate John Latham defeated the Nationalist candidate in Kooyong, and in alliance with the new Country party holding the balance of power, ousted Hughes as prime minister after the 1922 election.

Hughes' replacement, Stanley Bruce, a businessman, temporarily reconciled the self-identifying Liberals to the new political order, because clearly Bruce *was* a supporter of the 'capitalist' system, and indeed, as an importer, a cautious sceptic of protection and critic of the working of the arbitration system. He was also a strong believer in the importance of rational policy analysis. But Bruce was a pragmatist. He was happy to adopt his party label for himself and describe himself as a 'nationalist' rather than a 'liberal'.

Bruce's main policy purpose was the development of Australia as a key project of the empire. As a supporter of the empire he was conservative, in his support for markets and competition he was liberal. He was determined to defend what he understood as the system of British liberty against its enemies on the utopian left, but he was above all a pragmatic problem solver and doer. He was a big borrower and spender for development purposes, not at all committed to the federal system, and willing to centralise industrial power in the Commonwealth. Menzies was later to say that "he [Bruce] was, of all the notable men I have been associated with, the most down-to-earth and practical, and the least concerned with either theory or rhetoric".[146]

Menzies' description of Bruce was an implicit criticism, because Menzies *did* see himself as a liberal, was a convinced believer in the vital significance of individual liberty, and was determined to defend liberal principles based around the value of individual freedom against

---

145 *The Argus* 26/10/22.
146 R.G. Menzies, *Afternoon Light: Some Memories of Men and Events*, Melbourne: Cassell, 1967, p.117.

both the militant left and the pragmatists who were now trampling the Liberal policy tradition, such as Bruce. What individual freedom might mean in a country whose government now restricted it in many areas of economic life would have to be defined. Menzies saw the decentralisation of power in the federal system as one of its institutional supports. He vigorously opposed Bruce's referendum to centralise industrial powers in the Commonwealth, and described the attempt to regulate workplace relations through the judiciary as "grotesque". In 1927 his father in law, perhaps reflecting a broader family view, was one of the former Liberals who established a new Australian Liberal Party. This new party declared that it supported "the complete and vigorous revival of Liberalism".

The new Australian Liberal Party, with an eye on its first target, the Victorian state government, which had just nationalised bus-services, drew on every cultural and philosophical support it could find, and declared an alliance between liberal and conservative ideas in Australia:

> Liberalism is more than a political creed; it is a gospel; it worships no meaningless shibboleths. Under it Conservatism, in its nobler sense, and progress, in its highest sense, go hand in hand. Conservatism has a mission – a lofty mission – to conserve the fruits of progress and to steady down hasty experiments that involve revolution without evolution, and bring countries and peoples back to their starting point, sadder and poorer.
>
> The humane legislation of Liberalism has everywhere made history, and with its humanity has been associated a fine healthy outlook on the material things of life. Capitalism has its defects and is capable of improvement. But Liberalism regards capitalism – so called – with its wonderful elasticity, its constant inspiration to endeavour and enterprise, and its ordered developmental genius, as the triumph of modern civilisation that only the blind and miseducated would seek to replace with the dead-weight and uninspiring limitations of those doctrines that would make every man and woman a State slave.
>
> The philosophy which professes a contempt for money is shallow. Money is a handmaiden if we know how to use it; a mistress if we do not. The parent who would advance the higher education of his children, the man who would buy a home, the couple who would go holidaying – all pursue these perfectly legitimate and praiseworthy ambitions in terms of money.[147]

The new party successfully defeated the Minister responsible for

---

147 *The Argus*, 25/1/27.

nationalising the bus services, the former and future Liberal Frederic Eggleston, but its real impact was to encourage the political ambitions of some younger liberals to enter the state parliament, Kent Hughes and Robert Menzies, who were determined to revive a more individualist version of political liberalism. Entering the Parliament as Nationalists, their strategy was to convert the Nationalists to liberalism, and their main vehicle to achieve this was to be a new party within a party. In November 1929, as the Federal campaign gathered pace, Kent Hughes, Menzies and T.S. Nettlefold set up an organization of young lawyers and businessmen called the Young Nationalists to attract young people with liberal individualist ideals into Nationalist party politics.

The Nationalist Federation conceded the Young Nationalists three representatives on its Central Executive. One of these was Menzies, who became President of the organization in 1931. In 1931 a journal *The Young Nationalist* was published, to be succeeded in later years by *The Australian Statesman*, which continued to be published through to 1945.

The Young Nationalists debated internally on policy directions, but on the whole *The Australian Statesman* was a vehicle for Menzies' version of liberalism. It was to show that a weakened but recognizable version of economic liberalism had survived. The Young Nationalists were formed at a critical moment in the intellectual debate about policy in Australia, when the first significant analytical challenges were appearing to Australia's decision to pursue a higher standard of living by isolating itself from international competition through the highest level of protection in the world (apart from the United States), and to secure the public interest and fairness through an expansive use of state power. It was a policy framework increasingly recognised as a destructive formula that the economist Edward Shann described as the strategy of "the hermit nation".[148]

Revival of Political Individualism

The revival of an individualist pro-competitive liberalism based around rational policy at the national level was ultimately a result of Menzies'

---

148 Shann, *Economic History of Australia*, p.ix.

political leadership, and the opportunities offered to that leadership by the failure of the economy to grow as hoped, its decline into depression, and the availability for the first time of extended analytical criticisms of the policy framework which Australian political leaders of the previous generation had built. Three such contributions stand out.

One was the Brigden inquiry into protection, established by Bruce and which confirmed his concerns. The inquiry found that there were no political checks to an infinite extension of the tariff. Citizens did not suspect that there might be limits, and that the "subtle complex of interests and patriotic emotion which creates willingness to accept further increases and extension of the tariff" was without restraint. "There is at present no influence to counteract the indiscriminate and indefinite extensions of the tariff".[149]

The economist Edward Shann wrote an economic history of the country in which he pictured the tariff as more damaging than drought.

> The increased costs laid on Australian industries by such policies are more deadly than those of drought. These have their compensations when the drought ends, but since federation there has been no breaking of the tariff.[150]

Australian manufacturing, which in the late nineteenth century had had much higher labour productivity than British manufacturing, in the 1930s was 30 per cent below Britain (Irwin,268). Shann had written, bitingly:

> The more the policy of a hermit Australia succeeded, the more surely would it bring slothful intellectual standards, and as a consequence, material decay, until, with scorn, some sea power from the world where necessity had maintained knowledge and energy knocked in the closed door.[151]

It was a mere decade later that Australia was attacked by Japan in the course of that nation's violent attempt to open markets and territory in China and Southeast Asia for its people and its industries.

---

149 Alf Rattigan, *Industry Assistance: The Inside Story*, Melbourne: Melbourne University Press, 1986, p.11.
150 Shann, *Economic History*, p.397.
151 Ibid, p.ix.

A third influential analysis was Frederic Eggleston's seminal *State Socialism in Victoria* in which he recanted a significant aspect of his liberal socialism and declared the failure of government ownership of businesses:

> I was converted from a strong advocate of public ownership of all common services to the view that under present circumstances the conditions for the successful public operation of many of these services do not exist in Victoria....From the personal point of view the experience was one of only partially successful resistance to intense political pressure from interested sections of the community, with practically no support from any political section or from the public....Nobody was interested but the "Interests".[152]

Eggleston's critique applied throughout Australia. The reason for the failure of these government-owned utilities was fundamentally a cultural one. To work, there had to be a priority given to the public interest over private interest. In Australia, with its individualist culture, that was to ask the impossible:

> There is much evidence that the reason for this failure is a failure of the individual citizen in his relation to the State; he regards the State as taking a responsibility off his shoulders, and he does not make up by any action in the way of co-operation or by discharging efficiently his political responsibilities for the relief which is given to him personally. Such a conclusion will probably be hotly challenged by the advocates of State Socialism, and for evidence of it the reader must be referred to the text. But if the conclusion is true, its importance must be recognized as crucial: it means that when the conditions have been made most easy for the individual and most has been done for him, failure has been incurred because of his failure to co-operate.[153]

In Australia's individualist culture, citizens took personal responsibility for matters that were under their control. They did not see government services as falling into this category. Eggleston's conclusion was that these services could not work to achieve a broader public interest, let alone fairness. As Hancock summed it up:

> Swarms of petty appetites attack the great common services for which the government has made itself responsible. A multitude of

---

152 Eggleston, *State Socialism in Victoria*, p.vii.
153 Ibid, p.13.

fragmented interests assail the common interest.[154]

In this fevered politics of the pursuit of private interests through the state, Hancock argued that the very ethical purpose of democratic government was being submerged:

> Sensible people say that a State should give up running businesses if it will not run them on business principles. Australian democracy has been taught to answer: 'But our State stands for something higher than business principles. It stands for ethical principles'. Herein lies the confusion. The end of the State is ethical – let us say 'the good life'; the end of the railways is economic – let us say 'efficient service at cost price'. The economic end of the railways is a means to the ethical end of the State. If the distinction is blurred, the railways become the prey of selfish interests snatching for advantages in the name of Justice; and the State, perpetually vexed and tormented with problems of mere living, is not free to take thought of the good life.[155]

In writing his book Hancock had had the opportunity to see Eggleston's thesis. He shared Eggleston's conclusion that what Australian policy-makers required was "a realistic individualism". So long as the great utilities remained in the hands of the state, they would be at the mercy of political pressure. "The strain upon citizenship is too severe. Mr. Eggleston sees no hope of salvation except in a self-denying ordinance whereby the State will divest itself of its great possessions. Let it leave the ownership and management of them to others, and content itself with its ancient function of guardianship and oversight in the common weal."[156]

These analyses were, in truth, devastating criticisms of the nation's political leaders, their failure to inform the public of the realities of policy, and the failure of the policy framework they had put in place, now supported enthusiastically by Labor and, with a sense of despair, by Bruce and the Liberals. It was a policy framework which simply did not fit the realities of the culture or economic life of the nation, however much the rhetoric of fairness, patriotism and nationalism were used to support it. It had collapsed as a result.

Through the Young Nationalists Menzies sought to revive the

---

154 W.K. Hancock, *Australia*, Sydney: Jacaranda Press, 1961 [1930], p.119.
155 Ibid, p.121.
156 Ibid, p.120-121.

responsible policy individualism that the disillusioned liberal 'socialist' Eggleston had called for. The President of the Young Nationalists T.S. Nettlefold wrote to the press stating:

> More and more thoughtful men must be coming to realize that leaning on the State will never get us through our difficulties. The cure for most of our troubles must be the effort, initiative and independence of individual citizens.[157]

The Young Nationalists discussed free trade, the failures of the state compulsory acquisition and marketing of primary products, and the dangers of Soviet central planning, now being recommended by some. The Depression focussed attention on the need to end excessive borrowing and public debt and balance budgets. And from a political point of view, most importantly, it provided the spur which would push Menzies into the Federal Parliament in 1934. Even before that he had taken an active interest in the formation of a new political force which, given Labor's determination never to be part of a multi-party national government, was the closest Australia could get to such a political mechanism to deal with the Great Depression, the United Australia Party.

Menzies played a key role in consigning the Nationalist combination of Hughes' Labor and the Deakinite Liberal Party to history, helped to engineer Lyons' resignation from the Labor Party, and bring him as leader into a new United Australia Party. Within the framework of that party which had the overriding mission of requiring Australia to live within its means, he defended civil liberties and sought to construct a system of voluntary National Insurance. But it would not be until his resignation as Prime Minister in the second year of the war, 1941, that he would fully articulate and refine his new individualist liberalism in his *Forgotten People* radio talks. It would not be until 1944, and the collapse of the United Australia Party, that he would establish his new Liberal Party of Australia, that would, he told its founding conference in Canberra, "revive liberal thought". He was to provide a quality of principled policy leadership that Australia had not experienced for decades, and it would

---

157 A.W. Martin, *Robert Menzies: A Life*, Vol. I, Melbourne: Melbourne University Press, 1993, p.78.

be an essential ingredient in putting an end to the mindless expansion of the Australian state, and the divisive rhetoric that was now sustaining it.

Controlling and Refashioning the State

Unlike Deakin, who had led a country where there were only the first glimmerings of university departments of economics, a public service that had few opportunities for the university educated, and was heavily dependent on the support of special interest organisations such as the Protectionist Association to run his campaigns, Menzies would come to office in 1949 with a political party whose platform reflected his own liberal ideas, was based on the membership of individuals, raised its own money, and was financially independent of special interest lobby groups. He would be able to work with a public service which had highly educated leaders who could provide him with public interest analyses of national policy, and he would be assisted by a small but coherent economics profession whose first fruits had been the 1930s critiques of a state bloated by debt-financed spending, utopianism and special interest privileges. He would also bring with him a more coherent understanding of the policy implications of the liberal tradition than that of any previous prime minister.

Menzies' main political opponents were the (conservative) interests that had been artificially created by the grant of state privileges and had dominated policy for more than two decades – protectionist manufacturing industry and the state-dependent trade union movement – while the illiberal forces of utopian socialism and international communism were still powerful within the trade union movement and the Labor Party. He received support from progressive businessmen in Victoria around the Institute of Public Affairs. He was thus fighting on two fronts against forces whose demands on the state for further extension were never ceasing. In his battle against utopian communism in the union movement he would have the support of the Catholic Church led by Archbishop Mannix whose anti-capitalism had at last been overtaken by his anti-communism.

Menzies turned out to be the right man at the right time for the revival of political liberalism in Australia. In addition to the factors mentioned above, he also had the advantage of significant changes in the international order. The disaster that protectionism had inflicted on world trade, and the conflicts between nations that it had fostered, were now in retreat before the new international framework arising from Bretton Woods and the General Agreement on Tariffs and Trade. He also had the context of a revival of individualist liberal thought internationally through the competing works of both Friedrich Hayek and John Maynard Keynes, whose microeconomic and macroeconomic policies respectively for the liberal economy would feed into Australia's public policies in a useful way.

While the major contribution of the new Liberal Party could only be made once it had won government after 1949, even in opposition Menzies used its platform to oppose a last-ditch attempt by the Labor Party to move Australia a further major step towards anti-competitive state monopoly through the nationalisation of the banking system, and the retention of wartime controls. Chifley's proposal to nationalise the banks was the opportunity Menzies had been waiting for to highlight the differences between Labor's utopianism and a rational democratic individualism. At a rally which packed the Sydney Town Hall to overflowing on 25 August 1947, Menzies reminded his audience that almost eight years ago he had declared war on Germany's fascist leaders: "Today I stand here in the name of the same free people to declare war on fascism in Australia..." He condemned Chifley as a man "who from the bottom of the soles of his feet believes in socialism, and means to put it into operation."[158] He detailed the way in which the government's policies on taxation and industry were eroding the enterprise system on which Australia's prosperity had been built, and placing the country ever more firmly into the hands of the bureaucracy.

In Parliament he described the *Banking Bill* as:

> the most far-reaching, revolutionary, unwarranted and un-Australian measure introduced in the history of this Parliament. Beyond question, the Banking Bill is the most important measure of a domestic kind ever to come before us, or before our predecessors in this House.

---

158 A. W. Martin, *Robert Menzies: A Life*, Vol. II, Melbourne: Melbourne University Press, 1999, p.71.

The mind at work in the Bill was not a democratic mind, but a fascist mind:

> The attitude of the Government is: 'We are the rulers of the land. We know better than the people what is good for them". That is the fascist mind.
>
> This debate, we passionately believe, begins a second battle for Australia, a battle in which victory will go to those who are not only brave, but alert and vigilant.[159]

Labor's further step towards state monopoly was halted by the High Court, which declared the Bank Nationalisation Bill invalid under S.92 of the Constitution. The spirit of Henry Parkes, the great advocate of the free trade clause, now reached beyond the grave, and placed in the hands of the High Court a capacity he had not contemplated. The High Court's interpretation of the "absolutely free" provision for interstate trade in S.92, now interpreted as a protection for freedom of enterprise, was a significant factor in preventing Australia moving down the path of post-war nationalisation as Britain was to do. This avenue for the growth of government, while not closed, was now judicially blocked so far as federal government monopoly was concerned.

In government after 1949, Menzies pursued the strategy he had outlined in 1942 to restore liberal government based on responsible individualism. The domestic politics of a direct and short-term face-to-face confrontation with the anti-competitive policies of tariff protection, compulsory arbitration and of White Australia he judged was impossible. He promoted none of them, but he did not announce repeal. Moving away from the politically managed economy was not easy, and Menzies himself was not an economist. His individualist liberalism came rather from his legal theory and his Scottish/Presbyterian background. The policy constraints against which Bruce and Lyons had struggled continued to slow growth. Menzies' liberalism was rather reflected to some extent in what he refused to do. From opposition and into government he refused to follow Britain down the path of continuing nationalisation. Nor did he follow Bruce into massive debt-financed development projects. His economic and financial aim was to revive

---

159 Kemp and Stanton (eds.), *Speaking for Australia*, p.142.

private investment and implement sound public finance.

Menzies' government imposed tight restraints on government spending and taxation. Australia began to shed its legacy of huge public debt. Public debt levels, which in 1949 had been 136.3 per cent of GDP declined to 51.9 per cent by 1966 (Menzies' retirement) and to 38.4 per cent by 1972. Taxation as a percentage of GDP declined from 25.4 per cent to 21.8 per cent by 1960. New government regulation of industry and society was restrained throughout the period of the Liberal/National coalition government, rationing was ended and remaining war-time price controls were abolished.

Regulation of imports and exports was actually reinforced by quantitative controls imposed in 1952, as a response to a balance of payments crisis, but these were removed in 1960. Their removal led once more and inevitably to an upsurge of industry demands for greater protection from tariffs. In 1963 the government appointed a committee of economists and businessmen (the Vernon Committee) to enquire into the workings of the Australian economy, including the impact of measures protecting Australian industry against import competition.

Menzies was much more comfortable waging war against cultural illiberalism. An early task he set himself was to change attitudes that had been encouraged by Australia's political leaders for three decades and more: anti-Asian racism, sectarianism and class hatred. He had argued in 1942 that the well working of Australian institutions required a great expansion in the middle class based on the extension of higher education to both men and women throughout the community. Liberal policies that encouraged self-reliance and personal responsibility would help to remedy the culture of dependence and reliance on others that had been fostered by the 'protective' policies of the parochial and divided nation Australia had become before the war.

Menzies' perspective on the social structure of Australia introduced a new dimension into Australian liberalism. It was a response to the artificial inflation of state dependent interests by the pre-war policies. The Australian middle class had been a by-product of the policies of economic freedom that had been pursued in the nineteenth century. In Menzies' view, its revival and expansion would provide the social foundation for a revival of the responsible individualism which a liberal society required. This educated middle class, he argued, would support rational policy and lift the quality of leadership in all institutions. One of his early initiatives was action to revive the construction of private housing and encourage home ownership.

The education policies of the Liberal and Country Party governments after 1949, particularly the widening of access to higher education in the universities and the development of more vocationally oriented institutions, changed Australian society and its politics in many ways. The new universities of the nineteen sixties and later, the Colleges of Advanced Education and the Colleges of Technical and Further Education, raised dramatically the educational level of the population.

The drivers of these changes were several, and Menzies – who viewed the expansion of higher education as the key to opportunity and to the middle class – seized the opportunities that the growing importance of science, technology and international developments presented. In December 1956 he established a Committee of Inquiry into the universities chaired by Sir Keith Murray, Chair of the British University Grants Committee. The brief of the Murray Committee was to "investigate how best the Universities may serve Australia at a time of great social and economic development within the nation".[160] Menzies was thrilled and excited by its report in September 1957. He described bringing it to Cabinet for decision as "an outstanding event in my life."[161] In his speech to the Parliament on 28 November 1957 introducing the government's decisions he set the proposed changes in their historic context:

> The social, scientific economic and industrial complexities of Australia today are largely beyond the imagination of forty years ago. Great skill achieved after high training is no longer to be regarded as something to be admired in a few. We must, on a broad basis, become a more and more educated democracy if we are to raise our spiritual, intellectual and material living standards. Viewed in this way, our universities are to be regarded not as a home of privilege for a few, but as something essential to the lives of millions of people who may never enter their

---

160 R.G. Menzies, *The Measure of the Years,* Melbourne: Cassell, 1970, p.85.
161 Ibid, p.86.

doors....This new charter for the universities, as I believe it should be, should serve to open many doors and to give opportunity and advantage to many students...[162]

Rising educational levels, as Menzies had predicted in his *Forgotten People* talks, began to influence all areas of policy and all the institutions of government.

From the establishment of the first Australian university by Wentworth in 1850, governments had drawn from time to time on the analysis of 'experts' in formulating policies, but the developments in higher education increased the opportunities for such consultation to a new level. 'Experts' increased from the tiny numbers on whom Bruce had drawn for his economic and social policies in the 'twenties' to substantial pools of knowledge and skill that could provide analyses on a whole range of matters, and which became available not only to government but to the universe of organized interests. The discipline with the greatest impact was, not surprisingly, economics, which was a specialized policy discipline, and focused on the development of intellectual tools of policy analysis. The rising tide of tertiary educated citizens created a new kind of policy lobby group, relying on a high level of analysis with an activist and campaigning orientation.

The area of social policy, interestingly, offered more immediate opportunities for politically acceptable individualist reform than economic policy. Menzies had a particular interest in the educational and health responsibilities of government, and while supportive of government investment was determined to end the discrimination against private activity in both fields. Soon after coming into office he established a voluntary health insurance scheme, and from the middle 1950s his government began to abolish restrictions on public support for private activities that conferred a public benefit as did private hospitals and schools, but were struggling as a result of heavily subsidised public systems.

The Hospital Benefits Scheme extended financial support to patients in religious hospitals. In 1952 Federal tax laws were changed to allow deductions for school fees up to 50 pounds. In 1954 deductions were allowed for school building programs. One of the constraints on

---

162 Ibid, p.86.

Menzies at this time was his life-long belief as a liberal in the Federal system. However an opportunity arose to establish a useful precedent in the Australian Capital Territory, which was under Federal government control. In 1956 the Federal government offered to pay interest on loans for capital works for non-government schools in the Australian Capital Territory. The private Australian Industrial Fund for the Advancement of Science in Schools was established in 1958 and Menzies was later to cite it as an inspiration for later government grants for science blocks.

Funding for science blocks was less open to charges of funding religion than more general grants would have been. It was also more closely aligned to the federal Government's concerns with national security and tertiary education.[163] The legislation was introduced in May 1964. Menzies also announced 10,000 non-means tested Commonwealth secondary scholarships. Menzies' liberalism based on non-sectarian policies and freedom of choice was beginning to supersede the colonial liberalism of a sectarian democracy.

During the war Menzies had protested against attempts by advertising to stir up race-hatred against the Japanese. In office he supported the development of trade relations with Japan, and through the Colombo Plan began to accustom Australians to the presence of large numbers of students from Asia. A massive immigration program broadened the perspectives of Australians beyond a mono-cultural Anglo-Saxon dominance. In 1967 the Holt government commenced the dismantling of the white Australia policy.

The report of the Vernon Committee recommended an increased role for government in planning for economic growth through the appointment of an independent Advisory Council on Economic Growth. In the still politically-managed economy of the 1960s, Menzies was unable to make the principled argument that government should simply allow the competitive market to operate in the interests of efficiency. Indeed, the word 'market' does not occur in his defence of the liberal economy. Nevertheless, the liberal spirit was alive and well.

We have ourselves, in pursuance of our own economic policies,

---

163 Don Smart, *Federal Aid to Australian Schools*, St. Lucia: University of Queensland Press, 1978, pp.72-74.

taken action now and then to reduce the demand for some particular commodities in order to meet some inflationary position; and no doubt any government would continue to do so. But to essay widespread redirection of resources within an economy to achieve some pre-ordained statistical result is a very different matter. It seems to us that the Committee has ... predicated a degree of planning and direction of the economy which in our opinion would not be either appropriate or acceptable in Australia...[164]

Menzies took the occasion to expound the link between his attitude to the report and his broader philosophy, as he "unhesitatingly" rejected the recommendation to establish an Advisory Council on Economic Growth:

In the Australian democratic system of government based upon the consent of a free community, no government can hand over to bodies outside the government the choice of objectives and the means of attaining them in important fields of policy, particularly when such bodies would, through the power of publication, come to exercise what I have described, I hope not extravagantly, as a coercive influence upon governments....[165]

Although Menzies' response was criticized at the time by academic economists, including Copland, and the report was defended by Sir John Crawford, Menzies' liberalism had provided him with the guiding principles that led him to reject policies that other countries would, in fact, soon abandon themselves.

The internal politics of the government impeded movement to freer trade. John McEwen, leader of the Country party and Minister for Trade, in charge of the Tariff Board, was keen to extend the Country Party's support amongst manufacturing industry and supported increased protection, even though the primary industries favoured freer trade. The employment of economic experts to advise the government on policy however paved the way for the dismantling of protection. Through the work of Alf Rattigan at the Tariff Board the vacuity of most of the economic justifications for tariff protection became evident.

During an era dominated by academic discussion of indicative economic planning, and the apparent rising economic strength of the

---
164 Kemp and Stanton (eds.), *Speaking for Australia*, p.180.
165 Ibid, p.181.

communist countries, Menzies not only held the line in Australia against the further expansion of the state, but introduced a range of policies to strengthen the relative importance of private activity, not only in the economy but in the provision of services. His strongly held views that individuals had the right to exercise choice in housing, health insurance, medical care, schooling, banking, media, and union membership were readily accepted by the individualist culture that had survived the era of political appeals to parochial nationalism, bloated government and utopian expectations. The anti-liberal statist attitudes embodied in racism, sectarianism and class conflict began to die out as Menzies brought a new tolerance to the nation's politics.

By 1972 there had been a major change in the Australian leadership culture and in attitudes to government that would be fundamentally important to the future shape of the Australian state. The special interests pushing for government discriminatory policies on their own behalf – principally, but not only, manufacturers and unions – were still strong, but the intellectual challenge to their claims had also strengthened, and the liberal philosophy of the dominant party gave force to the new thinking. In 1971 Australia's first Restrictive Trade Practices Act was passed that moved the legislative framework for the economy towards an explicit support for competition. Government spending had been restrained, the burden of public borrowing on the Budget greatly reduced, the principle of voluntary health insurance had been introduced, the schooling and health systems had been set on a new, non-sectarian and more competitive basis, the threat of some form of modified centralised economic planning had been repelled, trade encouragement had become a dominant policy consideration and the analytical questioning of whether there was any economic case for tariff protection had begun.

A referendum in 1967 had opened the way to national policies to assist in the advancement of the aboriginal people. The largest immigration program in the nation's history, and the dismantling of white Australia with the abandonment by the Holt government of the dictation test, presaged a new openness of Australia to the world. As democratic governments around the world were expanding their activities, Menzies and his successors had largely held the line, reinforced liberal ideas in the culture, and laid the political foundation for future developments.

The growth and education of the expanded middle class affected not only politics but the Labor Party, and paved the way for that party's abandonment of utopian socialism under Whitlam, and its acceptance of the need for the liberalisation of economic policies under Hawke. Menzies' strategy for the re-liberalisation of Australia, and for the placing of public policy on a more consistently rational basis had achieved the success that Australia's individualist culture and powerful liberal tradition had made possible.

The Whitlam Labor government (1972-1975) resumed the growth of public spending and policies of centralisation, but in the area of tariff protection it made a bold, if politically costly, blow against protectionism with a 25 per cent reduction in tariffs. Labor, despite its links to the union movement, found tariff reduction seemingly easier to undertake than the Coalition, with its then determinedly protectionist Country Party ally. The oil shocks and the growing influence internationally of liberal economists such as Milton Friedman paved the way for a further liberalisation of the Australian policy culture in the later seventies and early eighties, with the establishment of new pro-market think tanks such as the Centre for Independent Studies and the resurgence of the Institute of Public Affairs.

Government expert analytical bodies such as the Industries Assistance Commission were supplemented by the establishment of other similarly liberal agencies to advise on agriculture and rural policy. Malcolm Fraser reined in the growth of government spending once again, and began to introduce greater flexibility into the management of the exchange rate. An inquiry into competition in the financial industry was undertaken (the Campbell Inquiry), and the introduction of greater simplicity and neutrality into the tax system (proposed by the Asprey Committee established by the Whitlam government) came on to the agenda. By 1983 the liberalisation of the policy culture in almost every area except labour market regulation was already well advanced.

The Era of Economic Liberalisation
The failure of the Whitlam government in economic policy at a

time when liberal thought internationally (as well as in Australia) was achieving a new dominance, led the Labor Party to embrace high-level policy analysis based around international openness and an acceptance of competition as the main driver of productivity growth. When it came to office in 1983 Labor's traditional orientation towards expansion of welfare had been tempered by an appreciation of the value of spending restraint and cautious budgeting. Hawke campaigned on the need for deregulation to go beyond what Fraser had cautiously attempted. Within the Liberal Party there was also growing frustration at the absence of support for further significant tariff reduction, for rural and other industry deregulation, and for the deregulation of the labour market. The revival of free trade and free market views affected both major political groupings.

The years 1983-2007 saw an almost complete rejection of the policy framework that had been established before 1930. Though some residual elements of that framework persist, both State and Federal governments have moved quite strongly to liberalise government service provision and intensify the competitive drivers for the improvement of productivity. Government enterprises have been privatised by both State and Federal Governments, including the sale of State banks and electricity companies, and at the national level the sale of Commonwealth Bank by the Labor Party and then of Telstra, the national telecommunications agency, by the Howard Liberal/National government. Tariff liberalisation proceeded with the support of both political parties through the 1980s, its direction symbolised by the commitment in the Liberal/National *Fightback!* document of 1991 to reduce tariffs to zero. Universities were freed up by Labor to participate in an internationally competitive market for higher education.

In 1994 the Keating Labor government introduced a national competition policy framework designed to encourage the deregulation of rural industries and the drawing into the market system of previously free environmental services such as water. This was continued by the Howard government. After 1986 the analytical attack on the arbitration system mounted, and following the Jobsback! proposals of the Liberal/National parties, the Labor government after 1993 began cautiously to strengthen enterprise bargaining. After 1996 the Howard Government revived individual contracts of employment in the form of Australian Workplace Agreements, and a major tax reform to simplify and increase the economic neutrality of the tax system took place with the introduction of the Goods and Services tax. The monopolistic Commonwealth Employment Service was replaced by a competitive service market for the job placement of unemployed people. Deregulation of the dairying and other rural industries, including attempts to deregulate the sugar industry, and free up wool and wheat marketing were made. Further liberalisation of schooling and health were undertaken, and importantly, the means testing of welfare payments was continued.

Liberalism and Conservatism in the reform process

The gathering pace of reform after 1980 was a product of the desire of Australia's political class to establish a policy process in which expert policy analysis had a key role. This analysis reflected the growing dominance at that level of liberal values shared across the elite political spectrum, but not of public opinion. Within the wider political culture, there remained support for many of the features of the old framework: government ownership of utilities, arbitration of workplace disputes, protection of Australian industries. It is not inaccurate to describe these as revealing a deep public conservatism and the difficulty of assessing the actual effects of policies, the residue of several generations of political leaders in the first half of the twentieth century who advised Australians to be afraid of the external world, to fear competition, and to aspire to a concept of nationalism which excluded the outside world. The utopian ideal of the hermit nation, weakened though it is, has refused to die. This conservatism found a political response in the 1990s with the rise of the One Nation movement led by Pauline Hanson, which reprised old attitudes to protection, against immigration and attacked aboriginal 'privileges'.

The appeal of One Nation was strongest in rural Australia and in those regions which had received fewest immigrants. It drew voting support from electors who had supported all parties, but especially from National Party and Liberal supporters. It can be interpreted as evidence of reform 'fatigue' as the nation opened up to the world and businesses rationalised in the face of competition in a way that had not occurred since the nineteenth century. John Howard recognised that if this conservative, indeed reactionary, movement was to be successfully resisted, it would be necessary to supplement the economic liberalism the party had inherited from the radical Hewson leadership with the overt defence, where practicable, of conservative values. For the first time in almost a century the Liberal leadership began to speak of a 'conservative' tradition in the party, as a way was sought to make the continuance of liberal economic reform politically acceptable.

The success of the new leadership policy strategies of the late twentieth and early twenty first centuries is plain. Real GDP per hour worked increased over 40 per cent in the years 1990-2012 as a result of both improved productivity and favourable terms of trade.[166] Large numbers of Australians embraced the expanded opportunities for choice in health and education provision. The economy began to operate effectively at full employment levels. Unparalleled access to choice of new goods, services and technologies was the product of openness to international trade.

The Australian story of the liberal reform of the state is one of the most remarkable in the world, and by 2000, having survived the Asian financial crisis without economic damage, the Australian economy, was being described as the 'miracle' economy of the OECD. It is hard to argue that it could have occurred without the acceptance, at the level of national political leadership over some seventy years, of liberal policy principles, and the eventual willingness of party leaders on both sides of the political spectrum to articulate a case for liberal reform. Among developed countries, Australia was almost unique (with the exception of the United States) in the commitment of all its major party leaders to policy liberalism, and to the institutional expressions of high level analysis on which rational policy could be based. It is argued in this paper that this reflects the profound depth of the liberal tradition in Australia from colonial times, in both its radical and conservative manifestations, and the continuity of an individualist culture that rewarded such policies

---

166 Patrick D'Arcy and Linus Gustafsson, 'Australia's Productivity Performance and Real Incomes', *Reserve Bank Bulletin*, June 2012, pp.23-36, 32.

with political success.

The substantial rejection by the Labor Party after 2007 of the liberal orientation to economic policy of the Hawke-Keating government showed that the influential union base of the party had not been won over to the new views, and that its leaders remained mired in the traditional approach of the trade union movement favouring anti-competitive and even xenophobic restrictions on the open economy, and persistent government intervention in investment and the labour market. The decisive defeat for this policy reversion in 2013, however, revealed that the forces pushing for liberalisation retained vitality.

The general sense of well-being created by the policy liberalisation up to 2007 was reflected in the results of a 2009 survey by *The Economist*, which ranked Australia first out of 33 nations on levels of trust, admiration, respect and pride in their country, with a score of 90 out of a possible 100.[167] Australia's stock of social capital might, by this measure, be said to be the highest in the world – giving Australians an extraordinary capacity to further lift the quality of their lives – if they knew how to do so. The match between an individualist culture and a policy framework that acknowledged the legitimacy of a society formed largely by individual choices had done its work.

Observations

There are a number of observations arising from the account in the paper.

1. The pressures for government action from special interests, including the sectarian advocates of religious and secular nostrums and utopias, never cease. Unless there is a political movement that understands this feature of liberal democratic government and possesses countervailing policy principles the risk of the expansion of government activity contrary to the public interest is high.

2. The content of 'radical' or 'conservative' ideas changes from one historical period to the next, depending on the institutions, interests

---
167 *The Australian*, 2/10/2009, p.8.

and values being threatened or defended. This is not to say that there are not some continuities of substance within 'radicalism' and 'conservatism', the most obvious being attitudes to authority. The authority relationship underlies all legitimate institutions in any human society. The theme of opposition to authority is thus prominent in radical political thought, while conservatism tends to defend existing authorities. The policy content of such radicalism or conservatism however depends on the society within which it is expressed. Detached from liberalism, conservatism can readily lapse into the mere defence of vested interests.

3. To the extent that we attempt to give meaning to the idea of a broad historical political 'conservatism' in Australia, it is probably most accurate to say that, in its attitudes to the role of government, Australian political conservatism has generally taken its colour from the dominant liberalism, though before democratic institutions were established in the 1850s political conservatism in Australia was also strongly influenced by the aristocratic aspect of English conservatism. The conservatism of vested interests has, however always been one of the main challenges to liberalism in policy.

4. The actual social and economic effects of government activity on any dimension are complex to understand in the absence of expert analysis (and even 'experts' may be wrong). Australian history shows this with startling clarity. Populist and popular policies to restrict trade and to privilege locals eroded Australians' standard of living and economic growth, weakening the country in the face of international aggression. Popular policies to redistribute income from competitive commodity producers through the wage/arbitration system made employment in dependent industries very vulnerable to fluctuations in commodity prices and to global depression. Government business designed to provide low cost quality services fell under the influence of special interests that increased costs and prices yet ended up being starved of capital, with consequent decline in service quality. More recently welfare

policies to help remote aboriginal communities by relieving them largely of personal responsibility for their economic welfare destroyed morale and came to be known by community leaders as 'welfare poison'.

5. While expert policy analysis has made a profound contribution to the reshaping of the Australian state over the years, especially in the puncturing of utopian socialist ideas, of the political rhetoric that justified protection, and more broadly in the reorientation of policy towards the encouragement of productivity growth through competition, policy analysis has always been subject to criticism on the ground that no analysis can deal with all consequences and can sound too 'theoretical'. This has, for example, been a common criticism by politicians of the analyses of the Productivity Commission, but such criticisms are merely current expressions of a long tradition of attack on analysis going back over two hundred years. Political parties will need to overcome their fear of 'theoretical' analysis and acknowledge their incapacity to implement complex policies without high quality analytical and evidential support.

6. The concept of 'big government' is an aggregate of different aspects, not well captured by one dimensional measures such as government spending, or levels of taxation or regulation. The shape of government activity changes over time, The members of the Australian public, considered as voters, have never taken the view that 'smaller' government on any particular dimension is necessarily better. It looks to government to deliver certain outcomes, such as employment and growth, opportunities, fairness and equity, personal and national security, and a sense of national pride and well-being. It expects government to achieve a balance between such general outcomes and the capacity of each individual person to make their own choices and use to the full their own life experience and knowledge. It accepts the state as a redistributor of income up to the point where taxes are seen to

be oppressive and unduly restrictive and perceived as interfering with the achievement of important private goals, such as home ownership, and the capacity to save for the future.

7. The role of political parties is crucial to the ultimate policy outcomes. Both Liberal and Labor parties were influenced by the rise of policy utopianism in the late nineteenth century, but the Liberal tradition had a stronger rationalist element, and a capacity to assess the economic and social consequences of policies beyond those that were the focus of Labor. Its philosophy of restrained government and secure individual rights was a better fit with the policy analyses coming from economics. The failure of utopian socialism, the rise of a substantial economic profession, and the success of liberalism under Menzies, led Labor to move from support for 'democratic' socialism to a philosophy of social democracy which can be considered as a variant of liberalism emphasising that government can have a positive role – not in fact denied by any variety of liberalism.

8. Australia may be the Western democracy with the most purely individualist culture. Its relatively recent mobile immigrant society, the absence of highly traditional interests and deep seated political cleavages calling on collective loyalties, has provided Australian governments with opportunities to develop policy frameworks supporting competition as a driver of productivity that are available to few if any nations, including the United States. It is suggested here that this is a central part of the explanation why Australia by 2007 had the freest economy in the world and one of the smallest of the government sectors of any advanced country, and has developed perhaps the most flexible and adaptive economy outside the United States.

3

The Progressive Conservatism of Alexander Downer: The Meta-Narrative of Resistance, Family Heritage and Edmund Burke

Paul Brown

> Progressive Conservatives could see the French system of government had to be reformed but not destroyed. We progressive Conservatives do not oppose change. The opponents of change are reactionaries. Progressive Conservatives recognize the inevitability of change *and the need to manage change in an appropriate way*.[168]

> I draw my intellectual heritage from Edmund Burke -- that is, a liberal commitment to a plurality of ideas and a the belief that there is no one way of social development.[169]

When W. K. Hancock wrote in his groundbreaking *Australia* in 1930 that Labor had assumed in Australian life the mantle of the party of progress and the non-Labor parties the parties of resistance he identified what would evolve into an enduring meta-narrative in Australian politics. Central to this argument was the assumption that social reforms had been the preserve of the Labor parties and that the conservatives had resisted changes at critical historical points. Under Whitlam this meta-narrative reached its zenith. Progress versus reaction found intellectual and political stereotyping in a postmodern cultural watershed in Australian politics. It would also prove to have

---

168 Adelaide Proclamation Day Speech, 28 December 1993, Glenelg, South Australia.
169 Alexander Downer, Minister for Foreign Affairs 'Reshaping Australia's Institutions of Diplomacy' Australian National University, Canberra, 18 February, 1998.

a determinative influence on emerging politicians such as Alexander Downer.

The use of this meta-narrative to label uncritically conservatives such as Alexander Downer emboldened Paul Keating to describe him in 1992 as "the idiot son of the aristocracy", a comment which passed almost unchallenged. And yet the lived experience for Downer was more complex than Keating's caricature, as can be seen by the progressive conservatism of his father and grandfather over three generations in beginning the dismantling of the White Australia Policy in 1958 and introducing female suffrage to South Australia in 1896. Post-World War Two historiography surrounding Australian liberalism has reinforced this teleology by failing to directly address it. Conservative histories conceived through the 'leader as hero' approach[170] had become personality driven and had not successfully questioned the initiative/resistance meta- narrative. Few leaders could match Menzies, and more nuanced studies attempting to hold back this teleology, such as the progressive conservatism of a long-serving policy maker as Downer, were largely ignored. It is as if 'the parties of resistance' had been successfully equated with the term conservative, which primarily meant reactionary, as those who were opposing change.

When Alexander Downer as Australian Foreign Minister refused to present the six volume collection of Manning Clark's History of Australia in 1996 to the Chancellor of Georgetown University in the United States it was symbolic of a wider intellectual struggle, a gesture concealing more than it revealed. Conservatism for Clark was conflated with the word reactionary; he described Menzies as "serving alien gods", "a tragedy writ large" who had failed to read "the direction of the river of life".[171] These distortions of treasured Liberal Fathers did not sit well with Downer's family heritage, in particular the role of Menzies as

---

170 See for example Gerard Henderson, *Menzies' Child: The Liberal Party of Australia, 1944-1994*, St Leonards: Allen & Unwin, 1994; J. R. Nethercote, *Liberalism and the Australian Federation*, Annandale, Federation Press, 2001; See also Gerard Henderson, *Why Menzies Matters*, Melbourne: Sir Robert Menzies Lecture Trust, 2008; and Judith Brett, *Australian Liberals and the Moral Middle Class: From Alfred Deakin to John Howard*, Melbourne: Cambridge University Press, p.183.

171 C. M. H. Clark, *A History of Australia*. Vol.6, 'The old dead tree and the young tree green' 1916-1935 with an epilogue, Carlton South: Melbourne University Press, 1987, p.496.

mentor. However the teleology of conservatives as reactionaries had commenced even earlier when Alfred Deakin described George Reid in 1906 as a reactionary wearing a "necklace of negatives" and this criticism was subsequently extended to the Nationalists and the United Australia Party.

When Menzies founded the Liberal Party in 1944 he captured this meta-narrative declaring:

> We have partly by our own fault and partly by some extremely clever propaganda by the Labor Party, been put in the position of appearing to resist political and economic progress. In other words, on far too many questions we have found our role to be simply that of the man who says 'No'.[172]

What then did Downer mean by his self-described progressive conservatism and what were the primary sources and influences for him in his personal adoption of this term? As a Burkean conservative, the equation of reactionary with conservative rankled with Downer and his evolving progressive conservatism, which was exemplified when as Foreign Minister in 1999 he successfully handled the East Timor crisis. His commitment to progressive conservatism had been forged from a family heritage of reform as exemplified in his forebears' attitudes towards immigration and female suffrage and the lesser known, but arguably equally seminal, rescinding of the 1910 Emigration Act in 1958. The repealing of the Emigration Act enabled indigenous Australians to leave the country for the first time without the requirement of special Government permits. This set in place a context for reform which would lead to the Menzies Government amending the Commonwealth Electoral Act in 1962 enabling Aboriginal Australians to enroll to vote in Australian Federal Elections and the Constitution Alteration Referendum (Aboriginal People) of 1967. The pivotal reforms of the 1910 Emigration Act however had been opposed by the 'parties of initiative' in 1958, by the then Labor leaders "Doc" Herbert Evatt and Arthur Calwell.[173]

---

172 R.G.Menzies Opening Speech, 13 October 1944, Conference of the Non-Labor Organisations, Canberra.
173 Arthur Calwell who returned Malayan and Indochinese war refugees at the conclusion of World War 2 against their will confirmed his position in his 1972 memoirs, *Be Just and*

Throughout his career the public statements and speeches of Alexander Downer consistently emphasised the imperative of sustainable change being legitimised by the wider community.[174] This was most clearly exemplified in his December 28, 1993 Proclamation Day Address in South Australia where he argued the case for progressive conservatism stating "We progressive Conservatives do not oppose change. The opponents of change are reactionaries. Progressive Conservatives recognize the inevitability of change and the need to manage change in an appropriate way."[175]

This statement is a direct reference to Edmund Burke and Downer's understanding of Burkean political philosophy. Burke held a talismanic position in his family heritage and Downer was now advocating that change needed to be introduced through what Burke called the 'prejudices', the enduring social and political 'habits', of any community. For Downer, the heart of progressive conservatism lay not simply in the content of reform as in the timing, sustainability and pace of the proposed reforms. As Australian Foreign Minister it was less a global ambition in practice and more a pragmatic geo-political resolution:

The second sort of regionalism is what I would call 'practical regionalism'. This is where regionalism achieves practical goals which cannot be achieved through the more general and relatively popular process of globalisation or indeed at the national level.[176]

In another response in February 1998 Alexander Downer as Australian Foreign Minister delivered a paper to the Australian National

---

Fear Not, arguing against non Europeans settling in Australia. He wrote: "I am proud of my white skin, just as a Chinese is proud of his yellow skin, a Japanese of his brown skin, and the Indians of their various hues from black to coffee-coloured. Anybody who is not proud of his race is not a man at all. And any man who tries to stigmatize the Australian community as racist because they want to preserve this country for the white race is doing our nation great harm... I reject, in conscience, the idea that Australia should or ever can become a multi-racial society and survive".

174 See for example Earl Page Lecture Armidale 2005, Pioneers Association Address, Adelaide South Australia,1993 and Alexander Downer 'Liberalism and the Challenges of Building an Open Society', 25th Annual Menzies Lecture Parliament House, Melbourne, 10 October 2002.

175 Adelaide Proclamation Day Speech, December 28 1993, Glenelg, South Australia.

176 Alexander Downer, Minister for Foreign Affairs, 'Reshaping Australia's Institutions of Diplomacy', Australian National University, Canberra, 18 February, 1998.

University entitled 'Reshaping Australia's Institutions of Diplomacy' which would prove to be predictive in the East Timor crisis which lay ahead. Anticipating changes in the Australian-Indonesian relationship Downer outlined a conservatism which he argued would produce "enduring" changes and create the "lasting institutions" necessary for countries such as East Timor. This conviction reached back to his most fundamental instincts evolved from both his family and educational influences in South Australia and England. Downer's paper subtitled 'Evolution versus Imposition-The Liberal Tradition' stated the rationale for Australia's involvement in East Timor should "evolve pragmatically in response to social development and need." When Downer asked DEFAT to conduct a survey with the East Timorese people in July 1998 he found eighty two per cent of the population did not just want limited autonomy but complete independence from Indonesia. This contextual imperative echoed his Burkean values and the call for local communities to provide their 'enduring authority' to act. Moreover it authorised the required justification for support to the East Timorese in their quest for national self-determination.

But where had this political philosophy been derived? Was it the product of his Australian Liberal Party involvement or something more fundamental? Whilst the East Timor crisis of 1999 was a pivot point in Australian foreign policy in the region it was also informative for what it revealed of Downer in a direct line back to his British educational experiences at Newcastle University and Radley College, Oxford. Downer's conviction that there should be a period of limited autonomy followed by independence was very much a reflection of his progressive conservatism. Downer stated in January 1998 "I draw my intellectual heritage from Edmund Burke -- that is, a liberal commitment to a plurality of ideas and the belief that there is no one way of social development".[177] He went on to argue that the imposition of political ideology over the interests of indigenous people cannot be effective as "this sort of hegemonic vision undermines equality of opportunity and diversity and in the end destroys democratic freedoms". Downer was essentially arguing that for countries and institutions "to be most

---

[177] Ibid, p.2.

durable" they need to "evolve pragmatically in response to social development and need." Rather than being an imperious government imposing values upon vulnerable countries in the Asia-Pacific Downer argued that his progressive conservatism could only be successful if it emanated from public opinion "sensitive" to "national sovereignty".

Again in the second section of his address entitled 'International institutions - Pursuing Common Value and Interests' Downer argued:

> It is not something which can be imposed from without, for if there is not the political will and the people with a knowledge and commitment to making those institutions work, then they will simply founder.[178]

The narrative which drove the approach to East Timor was steeped in 'practical regionalism' a direct application of the principles of Burkean Conservatism. Rather than being reactionary conservatism it was based on the tenet that "Australia's institutions of diplomacy must reflect the changes, the opportunities and vitality of the society and world around them."

Studying Benjamin Disraeli in British Conservative Societies in 1972 Downer observed the same challenge from a different historical perspective. Disraeli's Burkean conservatism appealed directly to the "customs" of a people for change:

> In a progressive country, change is constant; and the great question is not whether you should resist change, which is inevitable, but whether that change should be carried out in deference to the manners, the customs, the laws and traditions of a people, or whether it should be carried out in deference to abstract principles, and arbitrary and general doctrines (emphasis added).[179]

Alexander Downer has identified his British educational experience between 1964-1974 whilst his father was Australian High Commissioner to London as central.[180] Downer was immersed in studying the British origins of constitutional liberty completing a double Honours Degree at Newcastle University, England. If John Howard would prove to

---

[178] 'International institutions - Pursuing Common Value and Interests', Australian National University, 1998.
[179] Benjamin Disraeli Edinburgh 1867 responding to the British 1867 Reform Bill.
[180] R. Linn interview with Alexander Downer. National Library of Australia, Oral History and Folklore Branch Research, Oral TRC 6100/23.

be the adroit pragmatist leading his senior team, in the years 1996 to 2008 Downer was to become, with Dr. David Kemp, an intellectual of enduring importance for the Liberal Party. Downer's statement that "to understand politics one must first have a deep appreciation of world history"[181] reflected a profoundly-held intellectual belief in the political efficacy of the study of history. Unlike Howard who studied law without a liberal arts introduction and Peter Costello's training as a lawyer, Downer's British secondary and tertiary education, particularly in British History, brought a wider dimension to the Party not evident since the Menzies period.[182] Downer was the only Liberal in the senior leadership team with a secondary/undergraduate British education which directly informed his progressive conservatism. Rather than reading Australian history he was being exposed to the English struggle for the rule of law and constitutional liberty through the English Civil War, the Glorious Revolution of 1688 and the political philosophies of Edmund Burke and John Stuart Mill.

Alexander Downer has described his family political influences as seminal. In the forward to Sir Alexander Downer's family history Alexander Downer described this influence in the following aphorism "Man is an omnibus in which all of his ancestors travel."[183] The political and philosophical influences of Downer's father and grandfather need to be examined in some detail to appreciate the inheritance of his progressive conservatism. His father Sir Alexander Downer will be discussed first, followed by his grandfather Sir John Downer.

Alexander Downer refers his progressive conservatism back to his father's influence: he assimilated his father's Burkean approach to immigration reform of the White Australia Policy. And whilst his father's abolition of the Dictation Test in 1958 is relatively well known

---

181 Personal Interview with author September 5, 2013 Woollahra, Sydney. During this interview Downer argued that the defining experience of reading British history in England 1971-1974 through Edmund Burke, John Stuart Mill and Adam Smith had shaped his commitment to liberalism in Australian politics.
182 Whilst others such as Prime Minister Tony Abbott and Josh Frydenberg have Post Graduate degrees from the United Kingdom Downer is one of the last Liberals to have studied Secondary and Tertiary Undergraduate courses resident in College at English Universities.
183 Sir Alexander Downer, *The Downers of South Australia*, Adelaide, Wakefield Press, 2012, p.ix.

as the beginning of the end of the White Australia Policy, dismantled by Harold Holt in 1966, what is not is the watershed legislation reform he introduced in the repealing of the 1910 Emigration Act in the same year. The reform of the Emigration Act enabled indigenous Australians such as artist Albert Namatjira and vocalist Harold Blair to leave the country for the first time without the requirement of special Government permits. This set in place a context for reform which would open the way to the changes of the sixties including the Constitution Alteration Referendum (Aboriginal People) in 1967.

Prior to 1958 all indigenous peoples were prohibited from emigrating without permits. Downer's changes removed racial stereotyping and discrimination around this question. Labor Senator Clarey realised just how profound reform was, and welcomed the progressive changes:

> The third matter I wish to mention relates to clause 64 which deals with the emigration of certain aborigines. I express my pleasure at the fact that aborigines will now be freed of the restriction contained in the act of 1910 which related to the emigration of young persons and Australian natives. No restriction or interference will be placed upon such aborigines, as was possible under the old Act.[184]

Downer condemned the previous practice of pooling all indigenous peoples who applied for emigration in the same negative category. In other words, regardless of whether there was a restraint on one emigrating to another country as an indigenous person you were categorised with everyone else. There was no distinction made within the indigenous peoples as a group.

Senator Henty commented upon the significance of this breakthrough in the second reading of the Bill on 23 September, 1958 with the following observation:

> In regard to aborigines, the underlying principle of the Bill is that any aboriginal should be free to leave Australia if he is not subject to restrictions in the State or territory in which he lives; or if he is otherwise exempted by the Minister from the need to apply for an emigration permit.[185]

---

184 A. Clarey, Member for Bendigo, Australian House of Representatives, August 26, 1958, Migration Bill, Second Reading.
185 Senator Henty, Tasmania, Minister for Customs and Excise, Australian Senate, September 23, 1958, Migration Bill, p.521, Second Reading.

Downer was pioneering new reforms not only for the dictation test but in the treatment of indigenous people regarding emigration. This was pioneering legislation in 1958 and little noted for its formative role in crystallising expectations for indigenous reforms. Clause 64 of the Act ensured the breakdown of racial stereotyping of indigenous people in this area of emigration. Sir Alexander Downer went on to comment on the significance of this new provision; it enabled "the untrammeled immigration of aboriginals who are not subject to disabilities". Downer was well aware of his positioning as a Burkean conservative in arguing that "this again is an attempt to revise our law in accord with the changing attitude towards this difficult problem." Change had been authorised from the community or, as Burke would have argued, authorised by evolving 'prejudices' within the constituency.

The Downer achievement in immigration was as noticeable for its qualitative achievement as its quantitative success. Whilst the quantitative achievements comprising immigration, deportation and indigenous elements formed the nucleus of his success the qualitative nature of Downer's work has perhaps been underestimated. Downer was able to reach across the Chamber and work with Opposition members who were conscious of their previous failure to reform the immigration statutes but realised the necessity to do so. This was one of his central achievements: to create change without a sense of triumphalism.

Receding recognition is given to the fact that it was Sir Alexander Downer as Minister for Immigration in 1958 in the Menzies government who implemented the most comprehensive "overhaul of our immigration legislation" in sixty years where "every aspect of the immigration law has been carefully examined in the light of over half a century of experience".[186] It was a systematic review process setting in train a series of future immigration reforms including the abolition of the Dictation Test in 1958. He described the Test as "an archaic, heavy handed piece of machinery, in the category of those singularly ugly museum pieces of the Victorian age". Downer was newly appointed as Minister for Immigration in 1958. What was the nature of this immigration reform achievement and how did an Anglo/Australian conservative succeed in

---

186 Australian House of Representatives, August 26, 1958, Migration Bill, Second Reading.

abolishing the discriminatory Dictation Test to "give Australia the finest immigration charter that the world has yet seen"?[187]

In repealing 19 existing enactments and "omitting 24 sections of the present act" one may have considered in retrospect that Alexander Downer was acting under considerable pressure from the Labor Opposition of the time which was calling for fairer, anti-discriminatory changes the conservative Liberals had been hitherto reluctant to concede. However a closer examination of the debates around the Bill reveals a very different context; one in which the Labor movement had opposed the relaxation of immigration legislation.

Arthur Clarey, Member for Bendigo in the debate around the Second Reading of the Bill in September 16, 1958 explained why the Trade Union Movement had influenced Labor to resist changes to the White Australia Policy and was only now conceding changes. Clarey argued that their concerns centred on labour constraints

> It might be well to mention at this stage the attitude of the trade union movement. From the 1850's until the beginning of the second world war, the trade union movement was critical of immigration. But since the second world war it has taken the stand that if there is room and opportunity in this country for people to settle, they should be helped to settle, but always with the proviso that the policy, whatever it may be, shall not cause damage to Australia's economic structure.

Prior to the Menzies Government both the Curtin and the Chifley Governments had declined to abolish the Dictation Test. Arthur Calwell, Minister for Immigration 1946-1949, had refused to relax any of the major racial restrictions which saw a large inflow of European migrants and virtually none from Asia. While Calwell built a very strong postwar immigration program, it always preferred English, Irish, Scottish, Greek and Italian migrants. Calwell explained his preference for this 'Britishness': "My aim and that of the Government, is to make the word, 'Australian' mean all that it truly stands for to every member of our community. We shall try to teach the children that they are *fortunate to be British*, and even more fortunate to be Australian."[188] The active

---

187 Australian House of Representatives, August 26, 1958, Migration Bill, Second Reading.
188 Arthur Calwell, First citizenship ceremony held at the Albert Hall in Canberra in 1949, Australian citizenship: a chronology of major developments in policy and law. Michael

application of the Dictation Test ensured that Asiatic peoples were not given much opportunity to settle in Australia.

The Menzies Government's strategy was to promote a suite of legislation, including the Nationality and Citizenship Bill, 1958 which received faint praise from Calwell:

> In some respects I think the changes made in the act are too sweeping. There are one or two categories of persons in respect of whom the Minister should reserve some power to himself. He is assuming now, very generously, I think, that everybody who seeks Australian citizenship is well-intentioned and will act honestly and fairly towards this country. I am not so sure about that. *I have a certain suspicion about some of these people.*[189]

Moreover within the Migration Act debate the reluctance of the Leader of the Opposition Dr. Herbert Evatt showed further evidence that although Sir Alexander Downer was taking every positive measure for change it was without complete bipartisan support. Whilst Labor on aggregate supported the Bill, during the readings of the Bill it opposed some of the key measures including the complete abandonment of the Dictation Test.

In an exchange with Mr. Freeth, Member for Forest, W.A., Dr. Evatt[190] argued the Dictation Test should be kept as a backup measure to be used on limited occasions. He would not concede its complete removal contending *"The test could always be held in reserve."*

The second portion of this extract emphasised the rule of law and introduced safeguards to protect the arbitrary exercise of the Dictation Test. Downer stated that without an independent commissioner

---

Klapdor, Moira Coombs and Catherine Bohm, *Social Policy and Law and Bills Digest Sections*, 11 September 2009, p.6.
189 A. Calwell, Nationality and Citizenship Bill, September 17, 1958, House of Representatives, p.1318.
190 Senator Butterfield on Evatt's racial views September 30, 1958, p.703, Second reading: "I recall the time when Dr. Evatt criticised the fact that we allowed foreign language newspapers in this country. We did not ignore that criticism. The Immigration Advisory Council appointed a special committee to look into the matter. The committee found that there was nothing objectionable in those newspapers and that, in fact, they made great contribution towards the assimilation of national groups in the community. By enabling these people to express their opinions, their doubts and fears, in their own newspapers, the department gains an insight into their thoughts generally."

recommending deportation the current circumstances "are capable of the greatest abuse." Clause 14 of the Bill made it mandatory for a Commissioner to initiate deportation recommendations. Downer asserted in the debate that deportation "can only be by the minister on the recommendation of an independent Commissioner." The Commissioner himself "must be a serving or retired judge of the federal or state Supreme Court, a barrister or solicitor of five years standing on the high court or Supreme Court."

This was one of several "important checks" on the power of the Minister regarding deportation regulations. The Bill centered around three main areas: immigration, deportation and the emigration of children and aborigines. Throughout the debate over the Bill, Downer constantly referred to the arcane, "clumsy, creaking operation" which had resulted in "resentment outside Australia" and needed to be replaced by the "neat, simple expedient of an entry permit."

For Downer a "thorough overhaul" was required as the reputation of Australia had been affected and needed to be reformed with a "humanistic quality." In defending the changes to the Bill, Downer referred to his own experience of incarceration in a Japanese prisoner of war camp. He was outraged by the practice of placing those who might be deported "and cast into the most convenient gaol." The new legislation provided for detention centres instead of prisons. His experience by being incarcerated in a Japanese war camp led him to believe that gaoling someone who might have broken a statutory law was unacceptable. Downer commented in the debate "there is a compelling case for reform in the treatment of those one might call statutory offenders. I have given much thought to their plight, along with four other members of this Parliament I found myself in a comparable situation during our incarceration by the Japanese for several years of the last war." Downer argued that the "ameliorating effects" of this legislation "will place Australia in advance of any other country in the world."

Downer's progressive conservatism was leading him to make changes that he considered were long overdue in Australian society. As a Burkean conservative Downer considered the time was right for change. He stated that "since the existing legislation originated, there has been a great advance in social thinking throughout the world. Certain practices which would generally have been accepted fifty years ago are now questioned and regarded as matters for reform. So it is with these measures." Downer sought to implement his vision of "placing Australia in advance of any country in the world" not only through the largest single change, the abolition of the Dictation Test, but through a "liberalisation of the law" in relation to deportation regulations. Downer viewed this as a watershed for legislation forming a dividing line between the "ugly museum piece of the past" and this "finest immigration charter" not only for Australia but as a world benchmark. These deportation proposals were required to "humanise" Australian immigration law and provide "justice for the individual."

To build the case that he was in fact completely rebuilding the Act and not just tinkering at the edges, Downer presented five examples of the humanising of the deportation regulations. As previously stated it would now be necessary for an Independent Commissioner to recommend deportation to the Minister. The objective was to overcome the "extremely arbitrary" practice of government ministers acting without due restraint. Furthermore he provided five other examples to demonstrate that this was in fact a watershed in Australian immigration policy. The second example related to "the arrest of suspected prohibited immigrants." Under section 48 of the previous Act an officer was able to arrest an individual whom he believed was a prohibited immigrant "offending against this Act." He wasn't required to have a warrant for arrest and as a result the suspect would be incarcerated for any period without a time constraint. Clause 38 of the new legislation reformed this by insisting that within 48 hours the individual be brought in front of a "prescribed authority" to determine whether the individual should have his or her detention continued up to a maximum period "of seven days pending the Minister's decision as to deportation."

The third example proffered by Downer concerned the requirement to provide broader information and justification for the deportee. Under Section 14c of the existing Immigration Act individuals were often not given details of the deportation order as this was not required under the statute. Downer argued that this denial of human rights meant that "such a power, naked and uninhibited, could cause great injustice." It was reformed by necessitating under Section 39 that individuals arrested be provided with full "particulars of the deportation order." Furthermore should there be any claim for mistaken identity by the individual "he would need to be taken before an independent authority within 48 hours." Most importantly should the "prescribed authority" be satisfied that there doesn't exist reasonable grounds for the apprehended person to be held then he needed to be "discharged" immediately. Conversely, should the prescribed authority determine there were existing grounds for holding the individual he would need to be taken into custody but this was to be subject to the overriding "powers" of "the High Court or State Supreme Court" to determine its validity or otherwise.

The fourth area to ensure safeguards for the individual was Clause 41 of the Bill. Here Downer argued that the individual although not electing to contest the question of mistaken identity sought to oppose the alleged deportation altogether. Prior to this, individuals had often been incarcerated without the normal legal protocols. Moreover the right to obtain legal defence was not being practiced to the satisfaction of the Menzies government. Downer argued that "a hearing can of course already be secured by writ or habeas corpus or by injunction" but the complementary provision of providing a robust legal defense was not in evidence. Downer appealed in his argument in the first May reading of the Bill to the ideal that they should exist and that "all reasonable facilities for obtaining legal advice and legal proceedings" be afforded.

The fifth example Downer provided in his presentation to the Parliament for the "humanistic quality of this legislation" identified the need to have officers who intended to search "buildings, premises or vehicles" first secure the necessary documentation, in particular search warrants. The strengthening of the legal processes for investigative police meant that further "arbitrary actions" would be minimised by the need to obtain the necessary search warrants for "prohibited immigrants or deportees." Downer argued this was in contrast with the current law under section 14b "whereby an officer can do all these things without a warrant."

All these new provisions outlined represented a reversal of past policy. It jars when placed in the meta-narrative of the non-Labor parties as the resistors. The immigration story is more complex than that. Evatt and Calwell were not Whitlam and Cairns. Their old style British race patriotism was a social model which had not yet met the writings and speeches of Whitlam and Manning Clark. Controversial amendments to the Act, most notably the reform of the 1910 Emigration Act for indigenous peoples, met with considerable resistance from the Party of Progress.

Progressive conservatism for the Downers had the leitmotif that change requires a specific context if it is to be genuinely progressive and there is a need to "need to manage change in an appropriate way."[191] The consistent emphasis on the Anglo-Australian relationship involved British liberal institutions being reinterpreted for the Australian context. The model for this reinterpretation of the British contribution to Australian life had been Alexander Downer's grandfather Sir John Downer. Implicit in this 'Britishness' was the re-expression of constitutional liberty and the rule of law for Australia vigorously pursued by Sir John Downer through his work in the establishment of the Australian Constitution. This tradition flowed from John Stuart Mill's direct involvement with the establishment of South Australia as a 'free colony', his personal involvement with the South Australia Association in 1834 and the fact that Henry Downer had been a founding family patriarch in Adelaide, 1837. Significantly, progressive conservatism was a continuous element of the Downer family heritage and can be seen originally in the political life of Sir John Downer.

Sir John Downer's progressive conservatism flowed directly from the Benthamite origins of South Australia, which in turn reflected the seminal influences of the Scottish Enlightenment and John Stuart Mill. Alexander Downer later identified John Stuart Mill as of foundational significance in his British education at Newcastle University just as his grandfather had been influenced in the new paradigm of Mill's progressive conservatism being seeded in Wakefield's South Australia. John Downer was inextricably linked to this perception which South Australians had of their origins as "a place of enlightenment and

---

191 Adelaide Proclamation Day Speech, December 28 1993, Glenelg, South Australia.

opportunity."[192] Mill himself even contemplated migrating to South Australia contending the "colonial reformers," as they came to be known, were the protagonists of the liberal canon "battling against tradition and the political establishment."[193] What is even perhaps less appreciated is the considerable number of members of influential South Australian families during these formative years with whom Mill corresponded.[194] More specifically the liberal views of race emanating from this tradition influenced Downer's attitudes in areas such as immigration policy.

Even amongst Protectionists John Downer's position was unusual. The political consensus very much supported the Restrictive Immigration Act with such contrasting figures as Protectionist Edmund Barton and Labor Leader Chris Watson in furious agreement over the need to rebuff non-European immigration.[195] The other conservative group of the period the Free Traders led by George Reid were also in alignment leaving progressive conservatives such as John Downer out on a limb.[196]

Much of the Labor support for the Restrictive Immigration Act emanated from the movement's ambition to terminate the system of Chinese and Melanesian labour and to quarantine the living standards of its constituency. Melanesian labour was contracted at very low costs and in being so cheap competed directly with the higher wages of free labourers.

T.B.W. Higman has identified in his study the concerns of organised labour regarding immigration:

> The origins of the so-called White Australia policy lay in the racial ideology and labour movements of the late nineteenth century. Although British settlers had early expressed concern that the colonies might develop a subservient indentured class of Asian workers, it

---

192 J. Bannon, *Supreme Federalist: The Political Life of Sir John Downer*, Adelaide: Wakefield Press, 2009, p.6.
193 D. Bell, 'John Stuart Mill on Colonies', *Political Theory*, 38(1), (February 2010), pp.43-46.
194 *Ibid*, pp.44-48.
195 Together with Bruce Smith, the Federal Member for Parkes in NSW, the two represented the most strident opposition to the White Australia Policy in the debate over the proposed Restrictive Immigration Act of 1901.
196 Deakin in the second reading of the Bill advocated restriction on the basis "the Japanese must be kept out because of their good qualities, not their bad."

was not until the 1880s and the debate over Federation that Social Darwinist notions of racial superiority came to drive politics and immigration policy.[197]

Opposing both his own Party as well as Labor made Downer's stand even more conspicuous. The Labor movement headed by Chris Watson, who would soon become Australia's first Labor Prime Minister in 1904, forged a tradition in these years supporting restricted immigration. Some of the most robust support for the Restrictive Immigration Act in 1901 therefore came from the newly formed Labor Party.

In direct contrast Downer had no such constituency and indeed his contemporaries in the Protectionist Party such as Barton and Deakin did not support his following views:

> This is not an urgent matter in practical politics at the present moment. It is merely a political cry for the purposes of gaining kudos… I do not anticipate or fear any intermixture of races from any Asiatics who may come here.

To enable the Downers to build this family tradition of progressive conservatism, a tolerant, open South Australia would need to have first been created and "planned as a place of enlightenment and opportunity."[198] How did this "call to South Australia" arise for one such as Henry Downer in 1837 a tailor from Portsmouth, England to be attracted to it? Unlike the penal settlements of Sydney and Hobart, South Australia was conceived of as a fresh start for settlement away from the economic restrictions of England with no "convicted felons" allowed to be transported from Britain as part of its founding Charter. Wakefield had spent three years in Newgate prison and was not convinced that another settlement based upon penal servitude would be successful. Influenced by Britain's Poor Law Reforms[199] Britain's

---

197 B. W. Higman, 'Testing the boundaries of white Australia: Domestic servants and immigration policy 1901–45', *Immigrants & Minorities*, 22(1), 2003, p.1.
198 Bannon, *Supreme Federalist*, p.6.
199 Britain's Poor Law Amendment Act was introduced in 1834. Its main provision was to enforce workhouses as a precondition for any government support, "Except as to medical attendance, and subject to the exception respecting apprenticeship herein after stated, all relief whatever to able-bodied persons or to their families, otherwise than in well-regulated workhouses (i.e. places where they may be set to work according to the spirit and intention of the 43d of Elizabeth) shall be declared unlawful, and shall cease, in manner and at periods

colonial expansion provided the opportunity for enlightened social and political innovation. Supported by contemporaries such as John Stuart Mill, Wakefield formed the South Australian Association comprising twenty-one founding members which conceived of a colony based on a different land distribution model to that of Sydney and Hobart.

The combination of this systematic colonization model and the progressive philosophies of John Stuart Mill and the Benthamites created a new social and political order in South Australia in fundamental contrast to the Eastern Australian experience of convict settlement. Under the Wakefield plan the successful British institutions of parliamentary democracy and the separation of powers would be implemented, with the potential of a Western utopia. Given the social and economic problems being faced in England the proposed settlement represented a new paradigm of opportunity for British and European settlers to find a fresh start in South Australia.

Following the success of a series of publications, including his seminal 1829 *Letter to Sydney* concerning his proposed colonisation plans, Wakefield gained an audience of a new league of political thinkers who were prepared to support his proposals. One of these political philosophers, who proved paramount in legitimising Wakefield's blueprint was the soon to be acquired patron of Australian liberalism, John Stuart Mill.

Other than Edmund Burke, no political philosopher has exerted more influence upon Australian progressive conservatism than John Stuart Mill, but what is not perhaps so evident is his central role for the Downers and South Australia. The meta-narrative of conservative as reactionaries again fails at this point; Mill is suggesting not a new Britannica but an adaption of British liberal institutions for a new frontier. This is hardly reactionary.

The rapidly changing nature of English society resulting from industrialisation and urbanisation during the nineteenth century were demanding different responses from society's leaders. Political philosophers were being challenged to provide new solutions as England

---

hereafter specified; and that all relief afforded in respect of children under the age of 16 shall be considered as afforded to their parents."

was-overwhelmed with social and political problems. The timing and resistance to Britain's new Poor Law Reforms had proved decisive in Wakefield's proposals garnering new interest from a diverse range of stakeholders including the British Government.

Britain's liberal institutions and parliamentary democracy model were not in question: its capacity to cater for the urban demographic changes of the Industrial Revolution were just being overwhelmed. John Stuart Mill had commended South Australia as an alternative to Britain in an article entitled 'The New British Province in South Australia':

> We conclude by most strongly recommending this little tract to all who are interested, either as citizens, in the means of relieving the industry of their country from the evils of an over-crowded society, or as individuals, in withdrawing themselves personally from those evils.[200]

Mill was centrally concerned with the British Poor Laws Amendment Bill of 1834 and the fact that Britain's lower classes in their movement from rural to city existence were incapable of supporting themselves, owing to unemployment and minimal wages. Settler colonisation in foreign fields such as South Australia represented the "most feasible" opportunity, Mill wrote in 1830, to remove the "immediate pressure of pauperism."[201]

John Stuart Mill saw in the South Australian proposal a paradigm of opportunity for families such as the Downers to create a new England giving its liberal institutions a new canvas on which to express themselves fully.

Mill envisaged it in this way:

> Like the Grecian colonies, which flourished so rapidly and so wonderfully as soon to eclipse the mother cities, this settlement will be transformed by transplanting an entire society, and not a mere fragment of one. English colonies have almost always remained in a half-savage state for many years from their establishment. This colony will be a civilized country from the very commencement.[202]

Mill was arguing here that in a new context the British model adopted

---

200 J. S. Mill, 'The New British Province in South Australia', *Examiner*, July 20, 1834.
201 J. S. Mill, 'The Labouring Agriculturalists', *Examiner*, December 19, 1830.
202 J. S. Mill, 'The New British Province in South Australia', *Examiner*, July 20, 1834.

would "flourish" like ancient Greece providing the potential for the colonies to outperform the home country. Surveying Britain's colonial expansion, Mill could see only a piecemeal attempt to implement British social and political structures. His reference to "a half savage state from their establishment" is an oblique reference to the penal servitude model of prior English settlements. Mill was seeking to provide the full liberal model "from the very commencement" to provide security and stability to enable socially progressive reforms. With such rich beginnings future citizens such as the Downers would be empowered to anchor future social reforms in the success of the "transplanted" British liberal institutions. In his later years Mill would be critical in his support for British imperialism but in these influential statements in 1834 he was providing the philosophical fuel for the systematic colonisation model Wakefield was advancing. Moreover it was at a time when Wakefield lacked personal credibility and standing with the British Government after spending three years earlier in Newgate Prison.

Australian political historians have rarely failed to note Mill's influence on conservative Australian political philosophy. His positioning within Australian liberalism is totemic. However his personal involvement in the foundations of South Australia and political influence on liberals such as the Downers requires further elucidation. To fully appreciate Mill's influence on progressive conservatism one needs to appreciate the extent of his desire to maintain the complete suite of British parliamentary, legal and educational institutions by "transplanting an entire society" to South Australia.[203] Mill was not so much concerned with a preference for Englishmen as he was that *English liberal institutions* needed wholesale relocation to South Australia. Just as Edmund Burke had supported the American Revolution critical of the way in which Englishmen had failed to appreciate the American demand for "no taxation without representation", John Stuart Mill was arguing that the British system needed to be transplanted to the south as an integrated model for the new settlers.

Sir John Downer, son of Henry Downer, was twice Premier of South Australia (1885 and 1892) and a leading figure in Australian

---

203 J. S. Mill, 'The New British Province in South Australia', *Examiner*, July 20, 1834.

Federation and Constitutional development, but perhaps what is not as well-known is how his progressive conservatism informed these roles.[204] This found primary expression on two fronts, women's suffrage and immigration. Contrary to the stereotype of conservative Anglo-Australian protectionists, Sir John Downer was an outspoken advocate for female suffrage, both white and indigenous, and a fierce opponent of the White Australia Policy. Sir John Downer as South Australian Premier in June 1885 provided active and timely support for Dr. Edward Stirling's groundbreaking private member's motion, the Constitution Act Amendment Bill, with its concomitant reforms surrounding married women's property rights. This was not a conservatism to enable state wealth redistribution but a conservatism to preserve British liberal institutions which in turn would "guard" over liberal values.[205] In other words, it was progressive conservatism that would fight for "equal liberties", such as female suffrage and non-discriminatory immigration.

Downer was a product of his South Australian origins. This meant an Anglo/Australian hybrid of diverse but related influences including the political philosophies of John Stuart Mill, Jeremy Bentham and the liberalism of the Scottish Enlightenment. All these influences were captured by E.G. Wakefield in his unique blueprint for the new Australian Crown and chartered Colony. This was not unique to South Australia as colonists in Canada and New Zealand would also have to reinterpret their British origins and institutions according to context. Greg Melleuish has observed "this Britishness in Australia was, by definition, selective

---

[204] John Bannon former Labor Premier of South Australia 1982-1992 has identified the independent position of Downer: "He had high integrity and his independence stemmed from his combination of conservative values with a liberal approach. Today the attitudes resulting from such a conjunction might seem at odds but at that time they were seen as progressive and compatible. For instance there is no doubt of his Australian patriotism and vision of a great Australian nation but it was always in the context of the British Empire and his origins. He told his colleagues: *"I was born a South Australian but my pride is to have descended from Englishmen." Supreme Federalist*, p.222.

[205] Bruce Smith: "If I am right in laying down, as the fundamental principle of Liberalism, that each individual should have secured to him the most absolute liberty, subject to such restrictions only, as are necessary to secure equal liberty to all, then it follows that the state should take no steps to curtail the liberty of any class, merely because it will confer an immediate advantage upon another class, even though that other class happen to be much larger or more influential politically than the former." *Liberty and Liberalism*, Chapter Five, London: Longmans, 1887, p.243.

in its nature. But it was generally a Whig/liberal understanding of Britishness, one that emphasised the growth of freedom and democracy. But that did not preclude quite deep conservative instincts."[206] For Sir John Downer his conservatism centred around his commitment to the British liberal institutions he argued needed to underpin the Australian constitution and Federalism. At the heart of this "Britishness" was the belief that freedom and democracy would prevail against any perceived excesses or external threats. Freed from these constraints his progressive conservatism enabled him to enter into the debates regarding female suffrage confident the evolving Anglo/Australian structures would withstand radical change. The key to Downer's position was the speed and extent of the change.

In the Australian Parliament Downer advanced wide-ranging arguments against the apparent narrowness of the Naturalisation Act 1903. He was concerned that for half of his South Australian electorate one of the first results of the united Australia was that "citizens cannot rely merely on their State qualification" but must go through a "whole paraphernalia of formality" in order to have ratified "a citizenship of at least fifty years." He stated that this had produced considerable resentment against Federation saying that citizens in the state of South Australia were "cursing a Federation which is so little of a Federation as to bring about such results."[207]

In John Downer's Australia of the late 1880s native-born Australians for the first time were in the predominant. This demographic shift had also witnessed a commensurate rise in nationalism around a native born view of its own place in the Anglosphere. Writers such as Banjo Paterson and Henry Lawson found full expression in J.F. Archibald's *Bulletin* which was gaining considerable national exposure. Many of these ideas were nationalist, republican and anti-imperialist. This was being complemented by the rise of the Heidelberg art school of Arthur Streeton and Frederick McCubbin where, for the first time, Australian landscapes were being captured in the muted greens and weathered

---

206 G. Melleuish, 'Conservatism in Australia', Paper presented to the Australian Conservatism Conference, November 29 2013, University of Wollongong, p.2.
207 Senator for South Australia, Parliament of Australia, July 2 1903, p.1.

greys of the Australian bush rather than the blues and greens of a romanticised Europe.

Against this rising background of Australian nationalism John Downer was developing his liberal vision of Australia, but it was one grounded in a deep appreciation of Western constitutional liberty which for Downer meant Britain. His dream was of an expanding empire of English-speaking peoples within what Neville Meaney has described[208] as "a certain Britishness" where the Anglosphere is being extended, not just the British nation. All of this is a clear echo of his South Australian progenitor John Stuart Mill.

It is important to contrast this endorsement of the *Australian* English with the emerging nationalism of the Australian Legend[209] evidenced in other writings of the *Bulletin*. If the *Bulletin* through Lawson and the parallel Heidelberg School would promulgate the meta-narrative of the non-Labor parties as the forces of resistance then the Downers would be the faithful custodians of the progressive conservative tradition: the Australian English. A progressive conservatism which would be pursued even more vigorously by his grandson.

When Alexander Downer flew back into Sydney from the United Kingdom eleven years after he had left on the Fairstar in April 1964 he found a divided nation. Mainstream Australia had voted heavily against the Whitlam Government in the December 1975 election with the Coalition securing a majority on their own of sixty-eight seats and the largest majority government in Australian history since 1949 on a two-party preferred swing of 7.4 percent. This result followed the November 11 Dismissal and whilst mainstream Australians had turned away from the uncompromising progressivism of the Whitlam Government the role of the Fraser Conservative Government in resisting the progressive Whitlam had only galvanised the initiative/resistance meta-narrative. The fusion of the dark, lost years of Menzies, "the dead hand of the

---

208 Neville Meaney, 'Britishness and Australia: Some reflections', *The Journal of Imperial and Commonwealth History*, 31(2), (2003), p.125.
209 For a revised discussion by Russel Ward of the debate and challenge of Humphrey McQueen see R. Ward, 'Australian legend revisited', *Historical Studies*, 18(71), (1978).

past"[210] and the perceived electoral arrogance of the Fraser Government ignited the long burning fuse of the culture wars.

Alexander Downer would commence a diplomatic career in 1976 before becoming adviser to Malcolm Fraser and then Andrew Peacock and the inaugural Federal Member for Mayo in 1984. However his preferences for the constitutional liberty arguments of Edmund Burke, the free market economics of Adam Smith and the liberal thinking of John Stuart Mill would see him stereotyped by this meta-narrative. His achievements would now be increasingly interpreted through the prism of racism, sexism and classism rather than the progressive conservatism of the Downers and their Western faith in the creative ability of the individual.

---

210 Clark, *History of Australia*, Vol. 6, p.496.

4

Conservatism in Australia

Greg Melleuish

It would seem to be a truth universally acknowledged that Australians do not want to be known as conservatives. They much prefer to be known as liberals. Unlike the United Kingdom and Canada, Australia does not possess a political party with Conservative in its title. There seems to be something about the word conservative which is not attractive to many Australians. They would seem to be more focused on moving towards a better future than in conserving what is best about what has come before.

Yet such a description nowhere near describes the reality of the Australian situation. It may be what some people want to believe, but to ignore the conservative element of Australian culture is to reduce Australian history and political culture to a caricature such as is found expressed in the famous, and some might say notorious, idea of the 'party of progress' versus the 'party of resistance' model of Australian political history.[211] The idea that one side of politics is always on the side of change and progress and the other devoted to resisting change may make for good political rhetoric but is useless as a tool of historical analysis. Reality is always more complex, and more interesting, than the models which human beings create in their attempts to capture it in words. Consider these two apparently contradictory aspects of Australian history:

- There has never really been an established church in Australia, or an institutionalised aristocracy. Australia would appear to have thrown off any legacies from the *ancien régime*.
- However monarchy has long been popular in Australia,

---

211 Its classic expression is to be found in W. K. Hancock, *Australia*, London: Ernest Benn, 1930, pp.197–238.

particularly at a popular level. Although Australia no longer has imperial honours, Australians can be seen as being somewhat obsessed with honours and titles and hierarchy, indicating a desire to recreate aristocracy in a new form. Tractarianism, a more hierarchical and traditional form of Anglicanism, has flourished in Australia. The radical Cromwellians, such as the Jensen brothers, are, in many ways, the odd men out. In fact, there is little evidence of Christianity in Australia throwing off the shackles of the past, unlike in America, and moving outside of the mainstream churches. In such matters they have demonstrated themselves to be surprisingly traditionalist. Being different has largely meant copying religious movements from America.

The reality is that there is a conservative instinct, or disposition, in any social order, even one's which like to portray themselves as being liberal, or more correctly, radical. This may seem to be a paradox but that is not necessarily the case. Conservatism rests on what Edmund Burke called a prejudice, the principle that if something has existed for a length of time then that is an indication that it possesses value. It appeals to habit and the desire to maintain the regular patterns of our existence. It can be observed that such prejudices are a common feature of the human condition, and can be found readily amongst academics who profess to be ideologically left wing and radical. In fact, most of what we believe is founded on an acceptance of authority rather than as a product of our personal investigations.[212] After all, who has ever seen an atom?

In any settler society, such as Australia was for a long time, there is an instinct both for change and a desire to preserve what has come from elsewhere. The bonds of tradition may be loosened but they are most certainly not discarded. Rather they are seen in a new light and treated differently. This may mean that settlers sift through the various traditions that they have inherited and choose, not necessarily explicitly but more through a process of elective affinity, those that they sense are most appropriate for them. In other words the nature of conservatism in a society such as Australia will be different to that of a metropolitan

---

212 Stephen R. L. Clark, *Civil Peace and Sacred Order: Limits and Renewals*, Oxford: Oxford University Press, 1989, pp.5-13.

society such as Britain. What is valuable to Australians, and believed to be worth conserving, will not always be the same as in the culture from which it largely derived its institutions. This is despite the fact that for a long time Australians desperately wanted to see themselves as more British than the British.

There are those on the Left in Australia who call their political opponents Tories, but the use of this term is artificial, almost quaint, as such a term has been rendered irrelevant by the fact that it refers to a context and a place which is not Australia. A similar point may be made regarding those who attempt to see Australian conservatives as local versions of American neo-Cons.[213] The conservatism of a country is *sui generis*; it is an expression of those things which the members of that country believes possess value, and which inform their prejudices.

It may be the case that the conservative instincts of a country such as Australia appear to be drowned out by the exuberance of those who emphasise what is new in a new land. This comes out of a desire to want to distinguish oneself from the metropolitan culture. But invariably what is new is but the flowering of a tradition which may have struggled in the old country. This can mean that what appears to be something new is often no more than a much older tradition dressed in a new garb.

What it is important to recognise is that in Australia there was no '1789 moment' such as occurred in France when the French decided to repudiate their past and to build everything, laws, government, church anew on abstract principles. Australians have wanted no more than the rights and liberties that they believed belonged to them as part of their heritage. There was no desire to break with the past. In this sense, they were quite similar to the American colonists before 1776 who similarly referred to their rights as those belonging to Englishmen in their struggle with the British government.

Hence, in choosing to be liberal, as indeed the Australian colonies did in the second half of the nineteenth century, they were not seeking to be radical in the sense of totally uprooting themselves and starting anew.

---

213 Niall Lucy & Steve Mickler, *The War on Democracy: Conservative Opinion in the Australian Press*, Perth: UWA Press, 2006; Norman Abjorensen, *John Howard and the Conservative Tradition*, North Melbourne: Australian Scholarly Publishing, 2008.

There was not, and never has been, an attempt in Australia to build a polity, a culture or anything else, according to the principles of naked reason. The Australian colonists were seeking to align themselves with a particular tradition of politics in Britain, the Liberal-Whig tradition, and to build on that tradition in the Australian colonies. Hence there was ridicule and scorn poured on the attempt to create some sort of landed aristocracy in Australia. But it is also clear that the advocates of an aristocracy, such as W. C. Wentworth and James MacArthur, were Whigs rather than Tories, and that the opponents of the scheme, such as Henry Parkes and Daniel Deniehy, harboured deep conservative instincts. They were not opposed to the British Constitution; they simply had a more democratic understanding of the nature of that Constitution. Parkes, for example, looked back to the Parliamentarians of the English Revolution; for him the British Constitution was inherently democratic.

So what did conservatism come to mean in Australia?

- Preservation of Britishness: the British tradition as understood by colonial settlers and the institutions of Britain, in particular the law, parliamentary institutions and certain traditions and customs that had come from the metropolitan society.
- Liberal-conservatism: the desire to limit what were seen as the excesses of democracy and popular government as can be found in John West's advocacy of federalism as the means of instituting checks and balances into colonial politics.[214]
- Religious conservatism: including the importance of a large Catholic presence that was not at ease with either liberal individualism or with the cult of Britishness.
- Over time the desire to preserve the forms of politics that had been established in Australia as an expression of a good political order.

In this paper I propose to examine one primary strand of Australian conservatism, which I have described as Britishness. In a way it encompasses most of the other forms of conservatism with the exception of religious conservatism. Britishness in Australia was,

---

[214] John West, *Union Amongst the Colonies*, Gregory Melleuish (ed.), North Melbourne: Australian Scholarly Publishing, 2001.

by definition, selective in its nature. But what it generally involved was a Whig/liberal understanding of Britishness, one that emphasised the growth of freedom and democracy. But that did not preclude quite deep conservative instincts.

This conservative instinct can also be seen in the desire to copy, as far as possible, British Parliamentary practice and procedure. It can be argued that the desire to emulate Britain became somewhat of a fetish for Australians in the nineteenth and twentieth centuries. It also provides an example of how the conservatism of Australia differs from that of Britain. The Australian colonies were granted responsible government, also known as the Westminster system, in the 1850s at a time when Britain was itself developing its system of government. Hence the mode of government of the Australian colonies was quite different to the idealised model of Britain that the Americans had used to construct their Constitution in the 1780s. It is probably correct to say that the Australian and British (and the Canadian) versions of responsible government co-evolved, which is why they exhibit quite significant differences.[215] The Australian colonies developed their system of government in their own fashion, even if they believed that they were following in the footsteps of the old country. The governments of the various colonies always resembled each other while being in many ways different from Britain.

The essential point is that the faith in things British meant that in seeking to conserve a British model the Australian colonists created something that was quite different from what existed in Britain. For one thing, British politics assumed a party system that was led by aristocrats who competed against each other for power. It was an aristocratic form of government. Despite appeals to ideas of natural aristocracy, responsible government in Australia took on a decidedly democratic hue. An essentially aristocratic mode of government, a mode of government which embodied a whole range of aristocratic mores and traditions, was transmuted into a democratic one, moreover a system of government that contained very little in the way of checks and balances. Colonial governments moved towards a form of democratic

---

[215] Gregory Melleuish, 'Colonial government', *Oxford Companion to Australian Politics*, B. Galligan and W. Roberts (eds.), 1 ed. Melbourne, Oxford University Press, 2007, pp.112-114.

centralism that could be justified on the grounds that the fundamental role of these governments was to provide the foundations which would enable economic development. The key role of a nineteenth century premier in Australia was to acquire funds from London banks to build infrastructure, especially railways.

In these circumstances there was justifiable fear by those who in the colonies we can label conservatives, but who invariably came out of a liberal background, that the form of democracy which emerged out of responsible government would be unchecked and tend towards despotism. John West had argued for federalism in 1854, in a series of articles signed John Adams, the great American advocate of checks and balances, because he believed that only a federal structure would introduce the sorts of checks and balances that were lacking in the sort of local democracy which would follow in the wake of responsible government. While West, as editor of the *Sydney Morning Herald*, spent some the years after 1856 until his death in the early 1870s in scathing criticism of the practices of democracy in New South Wales, his Parliamentary reporter Charles de Boos satirised the emerging democratic political culture of those years.[216] It is worthwhile noting that it was colonial conservatives, including West and de Boos and, in the early 1880s Bede Dalley, who spoke up on behalf of the Chinese and the protection of their rights against what can be seen as the excesses of democracy.[217]

Here we have a paradox. Despite the protestations of West and the obvious lack of very effective checks and balances, democracy in the Australian colonies never became as despotic as its critics feared. The effective reason for this state of affairs was that the desire to emulate Britain acted as a restraint on democratic excess. Britishness as an element of the political culture preserved aristocratic values of individualism, respect for leadership and superior ability and the desire that one behave in a restrained fashion. This may sound strange but it coincides with an argument made by Lorens Samons about Athenian democracy. Samons argues that Athenian democracy was saved from itself by the fact that

---

216 See for example Chas De Boos, *The Congewoi Correspondence: Being the Letters of Mr John Smith*, Sydney: E. R. Cole, 1874.
217 Robert Lehane, *William Bede Dalley: Silver-tongued pride of old Sydney*, Canberra: Ginninderra Press, 2007, p.232.

Athenian culture remained largely aristocratic in nature. Unfortunately, he laments, the same is not true of twenty first century America.[218]

Britishness, considered as the desire to preserve the traditions of the old country, was an effective conservative force in Australian political culture because it limited the potentially despotic and destructive impact of a democracy that would otherwise have been rootless and simply grounded in the contemporary political will. Britishness helped to ensure that utilitarianism did not rule the roost in Australia, but was softened in its impact. It should also be emphasised that Britishness in Australia must be understood not as some objective reality but as the creation of Australians as they actively appropriated traditions from the metropolitan culture. The only real problem from a wider conservative perspective with colonial understandings of Britishness is that the nature of Britishness was too often interpreted in a spirit of optimism which overemphasised the capacity for human improvement. This was natural in a nineteenth century British community which was devoted to economic development and progress as summed up in the Great Exhibition of 1851.[219] But without a proper appreciation of the darker side of human nature, a spirit of optimism was encouraged which led to Australians neglecting the need to create constraints, such as are exemplified by checks and balances, which would guard against human excess.

The conservative dimension of ideals of Britishness can be illustrated by the case of Sir Henry Parkes. Parkes was described in the 1850s as the major supporter of genuine democracy in New South Wales.[220] Although Parkes remained a consummate politician, perhaps the greatest politician ever seen in Australia, his speeches indicate a deep conservatism founded on his understanding of the British heritage. Parkes was a democrat who believed, for example, that voters should elect members of Parliament who were good English gentlemen.[221] For him, democracy was the true

---

218 Loren J Samons II, *What's Wrong with Democracy? From Athenian Practice to American Worship*, Berkeley: University of California Press, 2004.
219 Greg Melleuish, 'Beneficent Providence and the Quest for Harmony: The Cultural Setting for Colonial Science in Sydney 1850-1890', *Journal and Proceedings, Royal Society of New South Wales*, 1985, 118: 167-80.
220 *Sydney Morning Herald*, 26 May, 1859, p.4.
221 Henry Parkes, 'Speech at Public Dinner at Kiama,' in his *Speeches on Various Occasions connected*

form of the English constitution, the one that settlers should preserve as part of their heritage. He had a deep respect for British institutions, but his respect was based on a Whig and liberal view of English history in which liberty had triumphed over despotism.

There were advocates of checks and balances in nineteenth century Australia, ranging from John West to William Forster but they were largely ineffective in placing conservative checks on the form of representative democracy that emerged out of Responsible government.[222] Instead the biggest check on the possible excesses of democratic government remained the British inheritance, or more properly the way in which the Australian colonists came to imagine an ideal Britain. This helped to slow down, even if it did not prevent, the movement of Australian representative democracy towards consolidating and centralising power.

And, in some cases, this sense of Britishness abetted despotism rather than opposing it. It was deployed, for example, to attack the Chinese and as an argument to restrict Chinese immigration into the colonies. In this area, good liberals, including Henry Parkes and George Reid, but not William Forster or Bruce Smith, must plead guilty. Parkes stated clearly that he opposed the Chinese moving to Australia because they were not British.[223] Liberal conservatives who believed in checks and balances were far more likely to oppose the excesses of the anti-Chinese movement than the exponents of Britishness and democracy.

Nevertheless, I believe that it can be argued that it was faith in the British heritage that acted as the most important conservative break on the growing centralisation of power by governments which have been occurring in Australia since responsible government was introduced in the 1850s. It aided the cause of liberal conservatism because an essential part of that British inheritance was a doctrine of liberty and individualism. To be British meant to believe in, and to practice, a creed of freedom.

---

with the Public Affairs of New South Wales 1848–1874, Melbourne: G. Robertson: 1876, p.174.
222 See Greg Melleuish, *Two Traditions of Democracy in Australia*, Sydney: Australian Scholarly Publishing, forthcoming.
223 Sir Henry Parkes, Influx of Chinese Restriction Bill, *New South Wales Parliamentary Debates, Session 1881 45 Victoriæ 5July to 20 December, 1881*, (Sydney, 1882), p.95.

- There was an acceptance of the Burkean ideal of the trustee notion of representation.
- There was particular emphasis on the conscience of the Member of Parliament and the ideals of the 'independent member' and the 'independent elector'.[224]

Put another way, in the absence of institutional design which took account of the tendency for power to accumulate and which created a set of checks and balances, the major defence of freedom in Australia against the creeping power of the state lay in the political culture which Australians had inherited from Britain, the colonies understanding of themselves as being British.

Again, we end up with a paradox. The Australian colonies did not federate because of any great passion amongst Australians for the ideals of federalism. It was the only way of achieving some form of national unity. The irony is that the separation of powers created by federation led to a limitation of the power of the Commonwealth government which had not existed in the old colonies. This check on government power at the federal level can be seen as almost accidental and certainly was not welcomed by significant sections of the Australian community. For a long time the Australian Labor Party wanted nothing more than to abolish the states and their House in the Commonwealth Parliament, the Senate. In the name of democracy they wanted to centralise power in a single lower house. Such a concentration of power would have enabled radical legislation to be enacted in a relatively easy fashion.

A similar argument can be mounted with regard to the Senate itself. The Senate has become a check on the House of Representatives almost by accident because the method of electing Senators was changed and it became increasingly difficult for any single party to control it. The independence of the Senate is now touted as a great check and balance in the Australian system of government, usually by those who are opposed to the government of the day. But that independence is not

---

224 See P. Loveday and A. W. Martin, *Parliament, Factions and Parties: The First Thirty Years of Responsible Government in New South Wales, 1856–1889*, Melbourne: Melbourne University Press, 1966, chapter 2.

the consequence of deliberate institutional design. It appears that many Australians have discovered the virtues of checks and balances very late in the day.

One could argue that the history of the last one hundred years of Australian political history has been the story of the ever growing power of the Commonwealth government at the expense of the states. There has been very little will to resist this process which has occurred largely outside the formal process of changing the Constitution, referendum, and has been achieved by such means as judicial review by the High Court. It has also been the story, especially during the past fifty years, of the decline of Britishness as a significant component of Australian political culture, and with that, the decline of the major conservative impediment to the extension of central government power.

What I am trying to emphasise is that the Australian system of government, which has its roots in Responsible government, has a natural tendency to centralise power and to create what I have elsewhere termed democratic despotism. Federalism provides a check on that centralisation, but because Australians have never been genuine believers in federalism, it has only slowed down that centralisation. The other check on centralisation has been inherited British traditions of political culture which impeded the growth of democratic despotism because those traditions emphasised aristocratic values. No one exemplified the restraint of Britishness, or its aristocratic dimension, better than Sir Robert Menzies, a liberal conservative who wished to conserve freedom and whose aristocratic values can be seen in his belief in the role of the traditional university and the need to extend the benefits of a university education. Menzies was very much what the nineteenth century termed a 'natural aristocrat'.

I have noted elsewhere that the decline of Britishness in Australian culture has created somewhat of a crisis for conservatism in Australia.[225] Australian nationalism may replace it in a way but from a conservative perspective Australian nationalism is problematic as it grew up in tandem with centralisation. It is not a nationalism that incorporates federalism or a respect for local difference; nor, unlike America, is it rooted in a

---

225 Greg Melleuish, 'Understanding Australian conservatism', *Policy*, 25 (2), 2009: 41-46.

faith in the individual and local community. It smells too much of the bureaucrat and not enough of the township. Conservative nationalists in Australia often evince too much faith in solving problems by using the magic wand of central power.

The collapse of Britishness has raised enormous problems for Australian conservatives who claim what might be described as the Burkean inheritance. Burke may be claimed as the first modern conservative but he was foremost a Whig and a liberal who understood that freedom should be embedded in the traditions that a generation both inherits from their ancestors and transmits to their descendants. He is the political patron saint of Australian conservatives, especially liberal conservatives, and his influence has been considerable across the whole Australian liberal and conservative spectrum. This can be seen in the nineteenth century in the almost universal adoption of the trustee ideal of representation by colonial liberals. This has been a defining feature of both Australian liberalism and conservatism in opposition to the delegate model of representation which was taken up by the Labor Party.

The Burkean mantle continues to be claimed in Australia up until our own time but the problem is: how does one appeal to a tradition that is slowly but surely vanishing? Over twenty years ago Ken Baker claimed that most Australians had not experienced genuine traditional institutions.[226] For example, British history has largely disappeared in our schools and universities, including the study of the seventeenth century English Revolution which was once so central to the teaching of history in Australia. A short time ago Tony Taylor rubbished the importance of the English Civil War as a topic of study for Australian students. He was answered quite correctly that in terms of our political traditions, including especially the growth of democratic institutions, the English Civil War actually does matter.[227] Sir Henry Parkes penned the following lines of poetry in the nineteenth century:

> Shall Cromwell's memory, Milton's lyre,
> Not kindle 'mong us souls of fire,

---

226 Ken Baker, 'Roger Scruton's conservatism', *Quadrant*, 34, 4, April 1990, pp.12-17
227 http://www.crikey.com.au/2011/01/31/memo-to-pyne-youre-reading-the-wrong-history-curriculum/: http://westerncivilisation.ipa.org.au/2013/08/architect-of-gillards-national-curriculum-attacks-ipa-over-english-civil-war/

> Not raise in us a spirit strong—
> High scorn of shams, quick hate of wrong?[228]

Australia may be the last common law democracy in the English speaking world but its political culture has evolved in such a way as to erode the foundations of its institutions. For a Burkean conservative, political institutions and political culture should grow together; the one should inform and nourish the other. Political institutions which do not grow in the rich soil of tradition have shallow roots; they tend to rot from within.

We can see the effects of this loss of tradition in Australia. There is the ever-growing power of the Commonwealth government as it seeks to control more and more of the lives of Australians. The Royal Commission into child abuse is an excellent example of the Commonwealth attempting to move into areas that belong to the states. But such things could not happen if both major political parties did not support the idea that the Commonwealth should be master, or mistress, in all things. Both the Liberal and the Labor parties view Commonwealth intervention, and if possible, control, as the panacea to a large number of the problems facing the country. The people of Australia seem to be happy to acquiesce when the Commonwealth seeks to expand its power. And on many occasions it has been the Liberals who have led the way. We would not be facing a national curriculum which undermines our Western traditions if John Howard had not got a bee in his bonnet about a national curriculum in Australian history. What is most disturbing is the way in which state governments do not seem to want to stop the national curriculum juggernaut. They just want whatever money the Commonwealth sees fit to dole out to them.

The great thing about Canada is that it does not have a federal department of education. There are benefits in having a Quebec which resists the centralising tendencies of a federal government. In Australia there is no equivalent force at work which can provide a will on the part of the states to resist such centralisation. The reason is as I argued above: Australians do not really believe in the federal ideal. Their political culture does not favour the proper workings of their institutions. They

---

228 Henry Parkes, 'Fatherland,' *Murmurs of the Stream*, Sydney, 1857, p.2.

are not jealous of their liberties and appear to be happy to hand over power to government.

Hand-in-hand with this increasing centralisation has been the growth of political culture that places increasing emphasis on human rights. For a conservative, particularly of a Burkean persuasion, the problem with human rights is that they are largely abstract in nature rather than being derived from the practices of a particular community. Moreover, in the contemporary context, they are often viewed as entitlements held by individuals or groups against the rest of the community thereby violating the liberal ideal of equality. The culture of rights would appear to be complementary to a world in which increasingly power is being vested in the hands of a government bureaucracy. Rights can be invoked both as a means of defence against bureaucratic excess and as a tool to ensure that the bureaucracy protects and secures one's entitlements.

Taken together, a culture combining abstract human rights and the growing power of the central government, a form of political culture which, it should be remembered, was created during the French Revolution and goes hand in hand with Jacobinism, is at heart fundamentally radical and anti-conservative. Now, one might simply say that such a culture is no more than a manifestation of Rationalism as described by Michael Oakeshott, the tendency of the modern world to assume that the only form of knowledge is abstract knowledge and to place traditional knowledge into the rubbish bin of history.[229]

But I believe that the particular political history of Australia has made the problem more acute in the Australian case. As I have argued, Australian politics and political culture from the 1850s to the 1960s invested very heavily in Britishness. Britishness was fundamental to Australian liberal conservatism. John West made an intelligent defence of the need for checks and balances following the American model, but one looks in vain for his intellectual successors. The colonists preferred to place their trust in their British inheritance rather than investing in the more abstract project of institutional design. In the early 1880s William Forster came to understand that a democratic lower house of Parliament

---

229 Michael Oakeshott, *Rationalism in Politics and Other Essays*, London: Methuen, 1962, pp. 1–32.

needed to be properly checked by an Upper House.[230] But it was too late. Democratic despotism had begun its long march.

The real problem is that the history of Australian politics and political culture has left conservatives with very few defences against the seemingly inevitable consolidation of power by the Commonwealth government and the creation of a politics founded less on practice and more on abstract understandings of politics.

Conservatives instinctively understand the ill effects of a politics based on centralism, bureaucracy and abstraction. This is reflected in the debates that have raged regarding elites versus the rest. They are debates that have a link back to Burke because he made similar critiques of the emerging elites of the French Revolution, the provincial attorneys, the men of letters and the scientists. Such men were the raw material out of which Jacobinism was forged. But understanding the nature of the problem and developing intellectual weapons against it are two different things. Conservatives can no longer appeal to the traditions of Britishness to defend themselves against abstract rationalism. Australian nationalism is not a satisfactory substitute for Britishness as it tends to be understood as in terms of increasing the central power of the state.

In the absence of a tradition of liberty founded on practice, what come to the fore are rationalist justifications for political action, primarily action by the state. This means loosening the restraints on the will of political leaders who are increasingly free to act on the basis of abstract notions and ideals of the good conjured up by their imaginations. In Australia this means an appeal to such things as efficiency, utility and creating a supposedly more rational way of doing things, what Hugh Collins identified as the utilitarian tradition in Australia.[231] It also means a growing emphasis on leaders as a manifestation of the democratic will. In Australia, as in other parts of the West, we are faced with an increasing democratic Caesarism which places far too much faith in the leader to 'do things' to protect the community and enhance its wellbeing.

---

230 William Forster, 'Upper Houses', *Sydney University Review*, 1, 1881; 'Upper Houses No. 2,' *Sydney University Review*, 4, 1882.
231 Hugh Collins, 'Political Ideology in Australia: The Distinctiveness of a Benthamite Society', in Stephen R. Graubard (ed.), *Australia: The Daedalus Symposium*, Sydney: Angus and Robertson, 1985, pp.147-170.

It represents the victory of nominalism over law, just as in early modern Europe the will of the leader, or absolute Monarch, all too often triumphed over established constitutional practices. This is one the reasons why the English Revolution should be studied. Political theorists such as Bodin placed the sovereign outside of the law because, as the source of the law, it needed to be above the law. In a similar fashion English theorists such as Robert Filmer and Thomas Hobbes supported the concentration of power in the Sovereign, especially the monarch, and attacked the notion of mixed government, in which power was shared between different elements of the constitution. In the English Revolution, Parliament sought to restrict the power of the King to act outside of established constitutional practices and to share power. The Glorious Revolution of 1688 created a constitutional monarchy because it put an end to the Royal prerogative and consolidated mixed government as the form of English government. Power belonged not only to the King but also to the Lords and the Commons. Judges could no longer be dismissed at the monarch's whim. In a similar fashion, as John West argued cogently, federalism, in an offshoot of England which did not have an aristocracy and lacked many local associations, through the separation of power between the two levels of government has a similar effect.[232]

And make no mistake, conservatism in a country such as Australia means respect for such long established practices as they place restraints on leaders who want to act in ways that they believe will enhance efficiency and prosperity but which turn out to be capricious and arbitrary. Constitutionalism can be a real pain for leaders in a hurry, but it is an essential safeguard against foolishness, 'clever' ideas and the excesses of an ego steeped in a sense of its own rightness. It restrains the desires of the human will which is too often guided by an over active imagination.

Any weakening of the foundations of Australian conservatism also means a weakening of its liberal traditions. It is possible to argue that liberalism can exist without reference to established traditions because of its emphasis on reason and because it seeks to go beyond the past. A

---

[232] Steve Pincus, *1688: The First Modern Revolution*, New Haven: Yale University Press, 2009.

tradition free liberalism is indeed possible, but it is the variety of liberalism favoured by the Left; it looks to abstract principles of efficiency and universal rights. It is the liberalism of the Jacobins who wanted to wipe the slate clean and re-build French society from the ground up: new constitution, new church, new legal code, new education system, new welfare system. We all know where that led with not just the Terror but famine in 1795 as they failed to create a new welfare system to replace the old one managed by the Church.

Liberalism in the Australian context has been the product of its British heritage; as mentioned earlier we are a common law democracy. The problem is that with the erosion of that heritage a new more abstract form of liberalism has come to the fore, one that increasingly owes much more to the Jacobins than to Burke. It can be argued that this combination of Jacobinism, democratic Caesarism and rationalism is a real challenge for conservatives in Australia. One can see its manifestation in some of the actions of the previous Labor government to limit free speech and to re-define the nature of discrimination. Personally I have felt for some time that we are living in an increasingly authoritarian society in which one is becoming less free to express ideas that are not officially sanctioned.

So where does this situation leave Australian conservatives?

A few basic points need to be established as follows:

- Australia has long ceased to be 98% British even if it ever was. Nevertheless our institutions are derived from Britain and have a British imprint on them even as they have evolved along their own path. Australia is not a genuinely multicultural society because it has inherited a largely English legal system. There is no desire to implement something like the Ottoman millet system in which defined entities run their own courts. In fact, over time, Australia has become less defined by a range of distinct cultural groups as by individuals who have mixed cultural ancestry. Cultural heterogeneity has not meant so much multiculturalism as a society which is amenable to abstract conceptions of law and government which have slowly come to replace concrete understandings rooted in inherited traditions. The end of Britishness in Australia does not

imply so much a move from monoculturalism to multiculturalism as a reworking of institutions based on Australia's British heritage so that they come to be understood in much more abstract terms.
- It is difficult, perhaps impossible, for conservatives to appeal only to abstract principles as the foundation of their conservatism. In any case, as has been argued, abstract liberalism is hardly a conservative doctrine. Nevertheless, conservatism has rational as well as empirical foundations, for example its view of human nature, but its emphasis is very much on the way that things work out in practice, and the need for practice to prevent the creations of the mind from running to excess.
- There have been attempts to construct a form of conservatism based on the conflict between the elite and its abstract ideas as opposed to the common sense of the ordinary person who conserves and preserves the traditions of the past through their practices. The best version of this argument in Australia was formulated by John Carroll. This position has some merit. Any democracy relies on a good relationship between its elite and the ordinary people and this relationship has, of late, become less than ideal. The non-elite does preserve its traditional understandings to a much greater extent than the educated elite which tends to be more deracinated and hence seduced by abstraction and imagination. But there is also the danger of this relationship being manipulated and turning into a form of populism that feeds into democratic Caesarism.[233]
- There have also been recent attempts to resurrect the ideals of Britishness in the guise of a more inclusive ideal of Western civilisation. Again, there is much virtue in such a project as Western civilisation ranges over much wider ground than Britishness, both in geographical terms and the areas of culture which it encompasses. This also means that it is much more abstract than Britishness; at times the West appears to float as a

---

[233] Greg Melleuish, 'Is Machiavelli or Tacitus more relevant for Contemporary Politics?', *Policy*, Vol. 28, No. 4, pp.39-44.

purely intellectual construct. That said, the West, understood as embodying a set of inherited traditions, makes far more sense in the twenty first century than Britishness as a source of values.

There is a need to re-consider and think through what conservatism, and by implication, liberalism, mean in Australia. Part of this involves a consideration of human nature. In his recent study of the relationship between conservatism and Evangelicalism in America, D. G. Hart argues that American Evangelicals need a good dose of Augustine to counter their tendency to see America as God's nation.[234] Australia is an entirely different case but Australians could also benefit from some Augustinian principles. To my mind this means that conservatives must argue for limitations on power and in favour of checks and balances.

The real answer comes as much from history as from reason. Many traditional principles have survived in the wider population, especially amongst those who are not part of the elite which has become addicted to abstract ideas. It is this group, as I see every year when I teach students who come from backgrounds which are decidedly non-elite, which embodies the common sense handed down from the past. This group appreciates instinctively the importance of Western civilisation as the foundation of the contemporary world. We need to provide opportunities for individuals to explore understand and absorb that heritage, always recognising that the past is indeed a different place. But then conservatism, as expressed by Burke and in its Australian manifestation, is not opposed to change or to reform, it is primarily concerned with the way in which change occurs so that it is orderly and does not discard those valuable things that we have inherited from the past. At the same time it is important that we do not idealise any particular group as embodying the 'good'. The 'people' also have a capacity for evil in the right circumstances; yet another reason for checks and balances.

Conservatives need to be able to point the past as a foundation on which they can take the present into the future, not as a plan but for the insight that it provides into the human condition. We need to recall Burke's famous statement that "Society is a contract between the past,

---

[234] D. G. Hart, *From Billy Graham to Sarah Palin: Evangelicals and the Betrayal of American Conservatism*, Grand Rapids: Eerdmans, 2011, p.220.

the present and those yet unborn." Part of that contract is ensuring that the present generation has a fair and unbiased view of the past as being composed of people like themselves, not people to be despised as criminals and degenerates. There are some simple principles that can be followed:

- Create histories that challenge much of the way in which Australian political history is told in such a way that Australia's liberal and conservative traditions are given a fair hearing.
- Demonstrate that the British and Western heritage is part of Australia's past and must not only be given its due but also that it was quite beneficial in creating a society of free men and women. Get rid of the endless, and mindless, negativity.

But, as I have already argued, it is not enough to appeal just to the value of the Western past. We also need a much more robust intellectual defence of all those important practices that limit the growth of government, which expose the folly of rationalist politics and impede the growth of the cult of the leader and democratic Caesarism. This means expounding the benefits of the rule of law, the importance of constitutionalism, the need for checks and balances, and, hopefully a proper defence of the value of federalism as a means of limiting power in Australia. These are, of course, all good liberal principles. But then, that should be obvious, because to be a conservative in Australia means being a liberal.

5

Australian Conservatives and the Politics of Science

Wayne Errington

Introduction
Conservatism is the most familiar yet most elusive of political traditions. Conservatives support different policies at different times and locations in pursuit of broadly similar goals – a disposition rather than a set of beliefs. This situational approach to ideology and politics on the part of conservatives can also be seen in their attitudes to science, at times defending tradition against scientific rationalism but approaching science in an instrumental way in the pursuit of other values such as health, national defence and economic development. The debate over climate change has placed science at the centre of national debate in a way that challenges political priorities in the economic, environmental and educational policy fields.

The chapter traces conservative attitudes towards scientific reasoning from the origins of modern conservative thought, and argues that debates over climate science reflect changes in Australian conservatism towards a more individualistic, ideological American tenor. While much of the focus is on political leaders, parliament and government, the aim is to trace broad patterns of thought and their adaptation to Australia's unique circumstances. There is a tendency for Australian critics of conservatism to focus on a particular set of contemporary issues as proof of some new form of conservatism, losing sight of the deeper and wider concerns for familiarity and stability.[235] Thus we

---
235 Greg Melleuish, 'Understanding Australian Conservatism', *Policy*. Vol. 25, No. 2, 2000, pp.

see unconvincing narratives of 'post-modern conservatism'[236] or 'neo-conservatism'[237] trying to make sense of the contemporary conservative resurgence. Indeed, conservatism's recurrent political success lies in its ability to make sense of new economic and technological realities and adapt accordingly. Not least of these in modern Australia is the preservation of a liberal society, constitution and family unit, providing conservatism with a closer relationship to the classical liberalism which it once opposed.

Understanding contemporary conservative attitudes to science requires attention to some of this history. Australian conservatives combine European and American intellectual influences with Australia's unique geographic and social environment. Part of the difference between Australian, European and North American conservatism lies in the unique settlement patterns and harsh natural environment of this country. The absence of a landed aristocracy has given Australian conservatism a different starting point from British conservatism. Yet, Australian conservatives have historically been more relaxed about state intervention than their American namesakes. Similarly, Australian conservatives have taken an instrumental approach to science, promoting its use in agricultural and industrial development. More recently, Australian conservatives have promoted market-based solutions to economic problems while underlining cultural tradition in response to new social movements and the post-materialism of the left. Attitudes to science have in turn been affected by these changes and by the anti-elite narratives popular on the contemporary right.

British philosopher Roger Scruton argues that one aim of conservatives is to preserve the 'social ecology', and that the 'material capital' contained in the environment should be conserved.[238] Scruton emphasises the way in which conservatives value the local, including their experience and use of the natural environment. The economic development of Australia was

---

41-46.
236 Geoff Boucher and Matthew Sharpe, *Times Will Suit Them: Postmodern Conservatism in Australia*, Sydney: Allan and Unwin, 2009.
237 Jim George and Kim Huynh (eds), *The Culture Wars: Australian and American Politics in the 21st Century*, South Yarra: Palgrave Macmillan, 2009.
238 Roger Scruton, *How to Think Seriously About the Planet: The Case For Environmental Conservatism*, New York: Oxford University Press, 2012, p.7.

enabled by state sponsorship of the technological means to master the requirements of transport and communication, as well as agricultural and industrial technology. While science and technology assisted in taming the environment, environmental science is now challenging commercial interests in forestry, the Murray-Darling Basin and carbon-intensive production. Liberal and National Party MPs are much more likely to dispute the reliability of climate change science than their Labor and Green counterparts.[239] The paper outlines the underlying philosophical reasons for these differences, and questions whether climate science is uniquely challenging to conservatives compared to other scientific disputes, and discusses the consequences of science being caught in the crossfire of adversarial politics.

Conservatiism and Scientific Reasoning
Shortly after the 2012 United States presidential election, the (very) early front-runner for the Republican nomination in 2016 was asked how old he thought the earth was. Marco Rubio replied, 'I'm not a scientist, man.' Most of us aren't scientists but in an increasingly complex world we need some way of processing debates informed by scientific research. Faith in science as an authority is widespread. Yet, most of us have ideals or interests that are challenged by the findings of science at one time or another.

Conservation might under the right circumstances be either a core conservative principle or a Romantic device in the way of human progress. It is common enough to observe that conservatism is not an ideology and that it owes its success to its pragmatism and flexibility. Where does scientific method fit into such a world view? Edmund Burke valued the knowledge embedded in tradition, essential for society's persistence but not residing in any individual mind. A more scientific strand of thought is represented by David Hume's empiricism. Science, though, can be a source of authority while being only one amongst others. Michael Oakeshott argued that the rationalist is "the enemy of authority,

---

[239] Kelly S. Fielding, Brian W. Head, Warren Laffan, Mark Western and Ove Hoegh-Guldberg, 'Australian Politicians' Beliefs About Climate Change: Political Partisanship and Political Ideology', *Environmental Politics*. Vol. 21, No. 5 (2012), pp.712-733.

of prejudice, of the merely traditional, customary or habitual."[240] He preferred practical knowledge and experience to technical knowledge, particularly if that knowledge was to be applied to the political realm.

Similarly, political and cultural conservatives are uncomfortable with any set of ideas, whether from left or right, bent on transformation of society or the individual. Not least when those ideas are dressed up as a 'science of society'. The criticism of Howard-era conservatism as 'post-modern' is grounded in the argument that the greater intellectual certainties of American neo-conservatives have influenced Australian contemporary conservatives more than Burke and Oakeshott's doubt.[241] While Australians have certainly imported some of the tactics of American neo-conservatives, this influence has been tempered by Australian and British traditions, as well as by Australia's unique political circumstances. Former leftists (the new in neo-conservative) gave American conservatism a greater sense of certainty. There were fewer of these fervent converts to the right in Australia. Still, the New Right project of the 1980s was not without its conservative critics who argued that change could happen too quickly.[242]

Conservatives support markets because of their efficacy, not out of some ideal. Conservative empiricism often leads to intervention to correct perceived market failures much more readily than classical liberals would prefer. This pragmatic approach to government is shared by the Australian public, which eschewed Hewson's market liberalism. While a long way from Hancock's notion of the state "as a vast public utility", Howard's success recognised what he called the "bedrock statism in the Australian psyche" when it comes to effective public schemes such as Medicare.[243]

Nevertheless, the influence of thinkers with greater intellectual certainty than Burke or Oakeshott is discernible in contemporary Australian conservatism. F.A. Hayek provided a crucial link between conservative and classical liberal epistemology with his critique of hyper-rationality,

---

240 Michael Oakeshott, *Rationalism in Politics and Other Essays*, New York: Basic Books, 1962, p.1.
241 Boucher and Sharpe, *Times Will Suit Them*, p. 72
242 Greg Melleuish, 'Conservatism in the 1980s', *Australian Quarterly*. Vol. 60, No. 3, 1988, pp. 305-07.
243 Howard cited in Wayne Errington and Peter van Onselen, *John Winston Howard: The Biography*, Carlton: Melbourne University Press, 2007, p. 228.

or constructivism – pointing out that markets work by dispersing the task of information-gathering, producing prices and quantities of goods more efficiently than rational planning.[244] Custom should therefore be respected as a repository of wisdom, even though Hayek didn't consider himself a conservative. Hayek feared that conservatives would appease the then-growing trend towards intervention in the economy rather than offer a distinct alternative. Oakeshott in turn thought Hayek too rationalist in his "plan to resist all planning".[245]

While social conservatives and economic liberals may have achieved a strong political alliance, their respective philosophical underpinnings leave important potential fissures. One such difference lies in attitudes to risk, and the application of risk to the natural environment. Individualists welcome risk. Conservatives value individualism but also respect hierarchy, which seeks to manage risk.[246] As developments overseas show, political conservatives might bend towards the scientific common ground on climate change or take a sceptical stance depending on the circumstances.

Socialists, by contrast to both liberals and conservatives, are risk-averse, seeing pitfalls in new technology such as genetically modified crops. From this point of view, there is risk everywhere in the profligate modern world, and solutions that rely on more and more technology present risks of their own.[247] In 2012, Australia saw an example of this in the debate over the super-trawler Abel Tasman, at first welcomed and then banned from Australian fisheries by the Gillard Government after a public outcry led by environmentalists. Scientific assessments of the merits of the case were easily dismissed by Green politicians. The different approach to this case and that of climate science is not arbitrary but governed by attitudes to risk and the role of economic development. Perceptions of risk will also vary depending on how close the observer is to the downside of the risk. While Australia's free traders bargain away quarantine restrictions in bodies like the World Trade Organisation, many

---

244 F.A. Hayek, *The Constitution of Liberty*, Chicago: University of Chicago Press, 1960.
245 Oakeshott, *Rationalism in Politics*, p. 21
246 Scruton, *How to Think Seriously About the Planet*, pp.72-76.
247 Marco Verweij, *Clumsy Solutions for a Wicked World: How to Improve Global Governance*, Hampshire: Palgrave Macmillan, 2011, p. 40.

farmers have a zero tolerance risk approach to imported food when one mistake could cost them their livelihoods. These notions of risk are part of a much wider constellation of 'cultural theory' developed by Mary Douglas and expanded by political scientists such as Aaron Wildavsky.[248] This cultural approach to political difference helps to explain not only the different political beliefs present in all political societies, but also why these different cultures mistrust each other, contributing to the adversarialism discussed later.

Science and Australia's National Development

The development of science in Australia contained a mix of individual patronage, civic institutions and state sponsorship already familiar in Europe. In Australia, though, the last of these was the most important, beginning with the scientific basis of Cook's voyages. Science was directed towards survival in a hostile environment. Sydney conservatives founded the Australian Museum and Botanic Gardens and colonial authorities held a tight rein over activities such as exploration and resource surveys.[249] Free settlers could see the advantages of such applied scientific activity. Universities were established as cooperative ventures but the teaching of science was usually sponsored by the state.

War, as it often does, increased state direction of scientific activities, and within Australia's federation, led to an increased interest in science at Commonwealth level. Billy Hughes encouraged the establishment of the Advisory Council of Science and Industry, which through various incarnations became the CSIRO in 1949. The application of science and technology to the state-led settlement of Australia has given conservatives confidence in many nation-building institutions, partly because, as Hancock noted, this state intervention grew hand in hand with an image of self-reliance.

Some elements of Australia's founding ethos, such as White Australia and protectionism, haven't survived the twentieth century. The place of other institutions in national life has also been highly contested in recent

---

248 See, for example, Mary Douglas, *Risk and Blame: Essays in Cultural Theory*. London: Routledge, 1962.
249 Michael Hoare, 'The Relationship Between Science and Government in Australia and New Zealand', *Journal of the Royal Society of New Zealand*, Vol. 6, No. 3, 1976, pp. 381-94.

decades. The expansion of education, while usually instrumental in filling the needs of the industrial and post-industrial economy, was built on principles such as excellence, uniformity and citizenship. Progressive educational theories built around individual discovery and creativity stayed on the margins for most of the twentieth century.

Thus the Menzies Government played an important role in the expansion of the university system. Boucher and Sharp contrast this record with a seven per cent real decline in tertiary education funding under Howard.[250] In between Menzies and Howard, Australian conservatives fell out of love with allegedly leftist-dominated universities. This view was promoted by B.A. Santamaria from outside the academy and Frank Knopfelmacher from within.[251] By the time of Howard's prime ministership, suspicion of universities was an orthodox position among Australian conservatives, seeming to take the views of those populating arts and humanities faculties as proxies for universities as a whole. The professional classes generally voted Liberal when these debates began in the 1950s, something that would change in the following decades.

Complementing this critique of universities has been the development of liberal and conservative think tanks. While these institutions are known mostly for their contribution to economic policy debates, some have promoted scepticism of mainstream science on a range of issues. The common theme in this scepticism is usually an accusation of overstatement of environmental or health problems that would require intervention in the market economy.[252]

A number of imported ideas were utilised in these debates – The New Class, the picture of intellectuals as an elite hostile to the views of ordinary people. As a political tactic, this is familiar conservative boilerplate about the right-of-centre parties standing with the majority of Australians. In recent decades, it is blue-collar workers whose social and cultural values have most closely matched those of conservatives as

---

250 Boucher and Sharpe, *Times Will Suit Them*, p.78.
251 Norman Abjorensen, 'The Culture Wars Down Under', in J. George and K. Huynh (eds), *Culture Wars*, p. 61.
252 Peter J. Jacques, Riley E. Dunlap and Mark Freeman, 'The Organisation of Denial: Conservative Think Tanks and Environmental Scepticism', in *Environmental Politics*. Vol. 17, No. 3, 2008, pp. 349-85.

the middle classes populated new social movements from the 1960s.[253] This trend was further enabled by the decline in sectarianism and the increasing number of Catholics finding a welcome home in the Liberal and National Parties.

Anti-elitism, though, can easily cross the line to anti-intellectualism, scepticism becoming cynicism. This is an easier mistake to make from opposition than from government. Howard, for example, had little choice but to accept the advice from the chief scientist, whom he as prime minister had appointed, about climate change science. From opposition, Abbott was indulgent not just of scepticism but outright hostility towards science.

The ability of parliament to wrestle with complex issues like climate change has not been aided by the narrowing of the backgrounds of MPs. The extent to which decision-makers have the type of experience and knowledge that conservatives value has been changing as the composition of parliament has changed. A number of Australians with scientific training historically gravitated to the conservative parties. So, too, plenty of people with practical experience in farming or other business have historically populated Australian parliaments on the conservative side. Representation of both of these groups, though, has fallen in line with the trend of every pre-parliamentary occupation being outweighed by employment in some political capacity.[254] Thus physicist (and climate change sceptic) Dennis Jensen was a lonely scientist in the 2010-13 Commonwealth Parliament. Interestingly, though, this fall in scientific literacy in the parliament may have little effect on debate over issues such as climate change, as I discuss below.

Outside parliament, the link between conservatism and the conservation movement was made increasingly difficult by the radicalism of the latter. Garfield Barwick was the founding president of the Australian Conservation Foundation. On the other hand, Malcolm Fraser's federalism outweighed his environmentalism in the case of the damming of the Franklin River. Consistent with Scruton's view of

---

253 Melleuish, 'Understanding Australian Conservatism', p.43.
254 Narelle Miragliotta and Wayne Errington, 'Legislative Recruitment and Models of Party Organisation: Evidence From Australia', *Journal of Legislative Studies*, Vol 18, No. 1, 2012, pp. 21-40.

conservatives valuing the environment on a local scale are programs like Landcare. When environmental concerns are national or global, local communities can be threatened by both the environmental degradation but also by the proposed solutions. Environmental activists and market liberals could both see the value in buying irrigation licences for environmental flows in the Murray-Darling Basin. The local communities set to be decimated by the buy-backs saw things differently.

With religion dominated by large traditional institutions, there have been few American-style battles over the school science curriculum in Australia. While some observers see the increasing influence of American conservatism in Australia including evangelical Christianity, the increase adds to a small base. Indeed, one of the more authoritative Australian climate change sceptics, the geologist Ian Plimer, was a slayer of Intelligent Design theories earlier in his career.

Conservative Attitudes Towards Climate Change Science

Margaret Thatcher's warnings about climate change reflected not only her conservatism but her scientific training. A staunch defender of the nation-state, Thatcher recognised the need for global cooperation: "… the problem of global climate change is one that affects us all and action will only be effective if it is taken at the international level." At a speech to the United Nations, she offered British assistance to efforts to understand the causes and consequences of climate change, and called for binding treaties to limit carbon emissions.[255] Once the scope of global warming and its potential effects became better known, contemporary conservatives have had to consider rhetoric about climate science and solutions alongside their defence of the economic system that may be contributing to its causes.

Thatcher was a woman of intellectual certainty. For conservatives steeped in principles of doubt, whose support for any economic or social arrangements is contingent on empirical demonstration of social benefits, the spectre of climate change raises difficult choices.

---

255 Margaret Thatcher, 'Speech to the United Nations General Assembly (Global Environment)', 1989, *Margaret Thatcher Foundation*. 8 November: http://www.margaretthatcher.org/document/107817

Dennis Jensen observes that "there remains the possibility that hitherto unknown aspects of the climate and climate change could emerge and lead to significant modifications in our understanding."[256] What to do, then about this perennial doubt over scientific conclusions?

As Tony Abbott has written:

> It sounds like common sense to minimise human impact on the environment and to reduce the human contribution to increased atmospheric gas concentrations. It doesn't make much sense, though, to impose certain and substantial costs on the economy now in order to avoid unknown and perhaps even benign changes in the future.[257]

The present costs of greenhouse abatement are known while the future benefits of action are unknown.

In 2007, John Howard had a problem. For years his government had accepted the science of climate change while only taking minor steps to control carbon dioxide emissions. The average Aussie voters beloved of contemporary conservatives respected scientific opinion on climate change and wanted to do something about it. It did seem like common sense to them. As it turned out the way to get an emissions trading scheme was to vote for John Howard at the 2007 election. Climate change played an important role in Abbott's replacement of Malcolm Turnbull as Liberal Party leader in December 2009. Turnbull's leadership was weak for a variety of reasons. Were it not for the Godwin Grech affair, Turnbull may have been strong enough to carry a fractious coalition over the line in support of the Rudd Government's Carbon Pollution Reduction Scheme (CPRS).

As the Lowy Institute Poll shows, by 2009 public support for costly action against climate change was well past its peak. The simplest explanation for the collapse in public support for emissions trading was that in spite of decades of discussion of post-materialism in Australian politics, economics still trumps the environment in the minds of the electorate. While voters might have approved of the idea of doing *something* about climate change, doing something that would cost them

---

256 Dennis Jensen, 'Accept It: The Science of Climate Change Isn't In', MP web site. 22 November 2010.
257 Tony Abbott, *Battlelines*, Carlton: Melbourne University Press, pp.170-71.

money in the midst of a global financial crisis where other states didn't seem likely to share the pain was a non-starter. Add the Gillard Government's lack of a mandate to persevere with a carbon price after the 2010 election and it is perfectly possible to conceive of support for carbon abatement policies falling without public confidence in climate change being affected.

Something more, though, was happening. The Lowy poll combines general attitudes to global warming with the costs that respondents are willing to pay to combat it. There seems little reason for belief in climate science itself to wax and wane. It is difficult to separate belief in climate science to a host of outside factors such as the lengthy drought or the global financial crisis. Psychologically, it is difficult to discount the priority one gives to a problem without also discounting perceptions of its seriousness. Something changed in the United States, too, where Republican presidential candidates Newt Gingrich and Mitt Romney were forced to back away from their centrism on climate issues in preparation for the 2012 primaries.

A number of reasons why conservatives might take environmental problems seriously have been discussed above. There are many reasons though, why climate change scepticism flourishes on the right. Climate change is one of a number of environmental problems that are global in their essence. The internationalist tenor of both the reporting of climate science, though the International Panel on Climate Change, and proposed solutions such as the Kyoto Protocol rile nationalist conservatives.

The nature of climate science, with its complex modelling and predictions into the distant future stretches the conservative sympathy for empiricism. As Abbott notes, "debate rages amongst scientists" about the projected extent of and consequences of warming.[258] Yes, that's what scientists do. The sheer volume of research fails to impress because it represents "one of the greatest public-good scientific cash cows ever devised".[259] Some scientists have been politicised by the public debate surrounding their work rather than any ideological hostility to the

---

[258] Abbott, *Battlelines*, p.170.
[259] Garth Paltridge, 'Science Held Hostage in Climate Debate', *Australian Financial Review*, 22 June 2012.

right. Many have a faith in rationality that lends them towards support for state-led solutions to climate change.

As overseas examples show, debates over climate science can lead to a variety of positions on the right of politics. Doubters might in some circumstances go along with a modest program of carbon abatement. The liberal rationalist and the hierarchical elements see climate change as a problem to be managed like any other. The British Conservative Party under leader David Cameron has taken this approach, though not without criticism from sections of both the liberal and conservative right. Unsurprisingly, in the United States, the more individualist culture of the right sees climate change something that a dynamic economy can adapt to. State-led solutions are simply opportunistic moves by the left to implement their preferred policy agenda.[260]

As a cabinet minister in the Howard Government, Abbott defended the position of doing something – if not much – about what the public perceived as a problem. While this remains Coalition policy, the individualistic US approach has always had some support in Australia, and has become easier to support as the costs of abatement programs becomes more clear.

Big business has been divided by interest, with mining companies and import-competing manufacturers concerned about costs on the one hand, and a more general concern about risk management and predictability of policy on the other. The sceptical cause has been galvanised by hostility to the Labor Government over the mining tax and workplace relations. Bjorn Lomborg's approach of accepting climate change science while critiquing the priority that governments give the issue is another avenue that has attracted conservative sympathy.

Abbott's concern about emission trading is partly grounded in a concern about "artificially created markets".[261] Further, as Malcolm Turnbull has pointed out, while the Coalition's command and control approach to carbon abatement seems more interventionist than an emissions trading scheme, it has the virtue (from the point of view of the sceptic) of being much easier to dismantle once the climate scare

---

260 Verweij, *Clumsy Solutions for a Wicked World*, p.48.
261 Abbott, *Battlelines*, p.172.

goes away. The 'climate-gate' affair, where a group of scientists sought to ensure that sceptical viewpoints on warming were more difficult to air in scientific journals, leaves plenty of room for those inclined to doubt the scientific consensus to do so.[262]

The distinction between doubt over the forecasts of climate science and certainty that the science is wrong is important, not least from the point of view of conservative epistemology. Given the interaction between discussion of potential costs of carbon abatement and our views about the importance of the issue, doubt – not certainty – plays an important role, even if that doubt is 'manufactured' by those with a vested interest.[263] However, the label 'denialist', with its echo of Holocaust denial, seems needlessly provocative, and typical of the cultural approach to climate change debate with which this chapter concludes.

Climate Change Scepticism as Cultural Adversarialism

The cultural element of the climate change debate begins with bedrock beliefs in either egalitarianism or individualism. Research that threatens these respective values is predictably enough processed with those biases in mind. The respective camps label each other 'alarmists' or 'deniers'.[264] Once the scientific findings become the subject of extensive public debate, we process the evidence with motivated reasoning – taking cues from participants in the debate from our cultural camp. The policy consequences of an elite consensus are not what they used to be. Through the internet the dissenters to any consensus can find like-minded souls. Without scientific expertise, there is more than enough scepticism circulating in the public sphere for those with an interest or an inclination to doubt the science to maintain their position. More and more results from scientific study won't convince either side once the contours of the disagreement are in place. Nor do higher levels of education or even scientific literacy matter much because cultural polarization is stronger amongst those with higher levels of scientific literacy.[265]

---

262 Verweij, *Clumsy Solutions for a Wicked World*.
263 Robert Manne, 'A Dark Victory', *The Monthly*, August 2012.
264 Verweij, *Clumsy Solutions for a Wicked World*, p. 1.
265 Dan Kahan et al., 'The Polarizing Impact of Science Literacy and Numeracy on

Nick Minchin provided one of the starkest illustrations of a cultural approach to climate change debate as he fought against Turnbull's bid to find consensus with Labor over emissions trading:

> For the extreme left it provides the opportunity to do what they've always wanted to do, to sort of de-industrialise the western world. You know the collapse of communism was a disaster for the left...and really they embraced environmentalism as their new religion.[266]

Evidence from the United States suggests that this type of rhetoric has an effect on trust in science on the part of conservatives more generally.[267] Minchin later appeared in a television program entitled *I can change your mind about climate*. At the risk of spoiling the ending, neither Minchin nor young environmental activist Anna Rose were able to change each other's minds about climate change.

The notion that political culture is important in climate scepticism is supported by the geographic variation of scepticism, with scepticism in the media much higher in the United States and Britain than elsewhere.[268] In the parliamentary Liberal Party, cultural conservatism seems a better predictor of climate change scepticism than does market liberalism.[269] There is no drier Liberal than Turnbull but his rationalism (and his lack of tribal opposition to Labor) caused him to look for greenhouse solutions along with the Rudd Government, much to Minchin's annoyance. The behaviour of many Australian conservatives during the climate change debate suggests a bias towards individualism and an appetite for risk more usually associated with American conservatism. This helps to explain why the pattern of liberal and conservative attitudes to climate science does not always follow what we would expect from the cultural theory approach discussed earlier. On this model, individualists like Turnbull

---

Perceived Climate Change Risk', *Nature Climate* Change, Vol. 2, 2012, pp.732-35.
266 Minchin cited in Sarah Ferguson, *Four Corners*. 9 November 2009. http://www.abc.net.au/4corners/content/2009/s2737676.htm
267 Gordon Gauchat, 'Politicization of Science in the Public Sphere: A Study of Public Trust in the United States, 1974-2010', *American Sociological Review*. 77(2), 2012, pp.167-87.
268 James Painter and Therese Ashe. 2012. 'Cross-National Comparison of the Presence of Climate Scepticism in the Print Media in Six Countries 2007-2010', *Environmental Research Letters*. No. 7, 2012, pp.1-9.
269 Waleed Aly, 'What's Right: The Future of Conservatism in Australia', *Quarterly Essay*, 37, 2010, p.90.

could be expected to eschew solutions to climate change since they have faith in humans to adapt to whatever conditions nature throws up.

The latter pattern is more obvious in the United States, where individualism and conservatism have a larger historical overlap. Similarly, Australian conservatives can effortlessly slip between climate change scepticism and the view that perhaps there is a problem but there's not much we can do about it. The propensity not to intervene to solve a possible future problem at the risk of harming tangible things like the mining industry governs such attitudes. However the notion that those pre-disposed to defend the social and economic status quo would naturally take a predictable position on climate change doesn't account for variation in climate change scepticism over time captured in the polling above and elsewhere. Indeed, it may be that anecdotal reports of coalition MPs responding to contact from constituents as they rejected moves towards a compromise over Labor's proposed ETS in 2009 reflected an important trend.

Minchin's point about the beliefs of environmentalists is important, as are their tactics in gaining support for their cause. Environmentalists target big business and the market economy more generally.[270] They tend to assume that all conservative opposition to climate change action is rooted in ideas promoted by the fossil fuel industry. This invites a more adversarial response from conservatives today than it may have some decades ago. Australia Institute head Richard Denniss has pointed out that a different approach from environmentalists may have been met with more cooperation from their ideological opponents.[271] Instead, doubt on the right was countered ever higher levels of ideological certainty on the left. Nothing was more likely to alienate the conservative mindset.

Scientists with an eye for a media headline and their gloom and doom predictions make solutions seem farther and farther away. Even the soundest of scientific research inevitably passes through the 'cyclotron of ideology' before it reaches the public sphere.[272] Accusations of 'post-

---

270 Scruton, *How to Think Seriously About the Planet*, p.7.
271 Richard Denniss, 'Green Groups Cop Blame for Sceptics' Rise', *Crikey*, 12 August 2012: http://media.crikey.com.au/dm/newsletter/dailymail_0b371b1b21eb690ed0a11556d104ee e3.html.
272 Scruton, *How to Think Seriously About the Planet*, p. 42.

modern conservatism' are easily met with accusations of 'post-modern science',[273] as sceptics make a meal of any question over climate science, as in the 'Climate-gate' revelations. The Commonwealth Labor Government established the Climate Commission with a view to promoting scientific knowledge to the wider community. Chief Commissioner Tim Flannery has long had his more outlandish predictions lashed by conservative commentators, making it inevitable that the Commission's role would be lost on at least part of the community. The desire to move on from debating science to finding solutions also antagonises sceptics, who question the entire notion of "settled science".[274] Still, as Abbott has written, "the fact that a green fringe would like Australians to live like the Amish doesn't of itself invalidate reducing carbon emissions as prudent insurance against possible future harm".[275] Indeed Abbott embodies conservative agonising over the issue. Prudence one moment, railing against "crap" science the next.[276]

Turnbull, as bruised by his loss of leadership as by the affront to science represented by the rejection of the emissions trading scheme, nevertheless has a point: "I think the denigration of science is a real threat. If scientists are mocked and derided, then soon we will have the total triumph of "know nothing"".[277] In many respects, though, the debate about climate change science has little to do with science and much to do with ideology, interest and adversarial politics. As obvious a target as the bloated polemic from an equally bloated Al Gore seems; as enjoyable as Tim Blair's satirising of Tim Flannery's hot air might be, cultural adversarialism is a poor substitute for traditional conservative approaches of gentle scepticism of all types of claims and a risk management approach to climate policy.

---

273 Paltridge, 'Science Held Hostage in Climate Debate'.
274 Bob Carter, 'Settled Science: No Such Thing', *The Australian*, 27 June 2012.
275 Abbott, *Battlelines*, p.171.
276 Abbott cited in Stewart Rintoul, 'Town of Beaufort Changed Tony Abbott's View on Climate Change', *The Australian*. 12 December 2009.
277 Turnbull cited in Lenore Taylor, 'Malcolm in the Middle', *Good Weekend*. 3 March 2012.

6

What I wasn't taught at High School

Chris Rath

With the collapse of the Soviet Union and global communism over two decades ago, the Left abandoned their belief in permanent revolution that would involve the proletariat around the globe uniting to overthrow the capitalist class. With Gramsci and Rudi Dutschke as their guiding light, the Left discarded their revolutionary tendencies to advocate for a slow takeover and perversion of Western Civilisation, known as the 'Long March through the Institutions'. It is a pragmatic and slow paced version of communism that was initially advocated in the *1963 Communist Goals for Taking Over America*.[278]

Stuart Macintyre, a former member of the Left Tendency Faction of the Communist Party of Australia, was the historian that was given the task of drafting the history component of Australia's National Curriculum. Perhaps it is too convenient that Stuart Macintyre has now softened his views to 'democratic socialism' and is part of the Labor Party elite.

I studied History at High School before there was any serious talk of a National Curriculum. However, even between 2002 and 2007, at a Catholic High School, the left-wing bias was noticeable. With a keen interest in politics and an admiration for John Howard's economically free market and socially conservative policies, I joined the Young Liberals in 2006 at the age of 16. I was young and impressionable, but I knew enough about politics to realise that both the content and the tone of teaching was severely weighted against Western Civilisation. Most of my school friends were not so discerning, preferring football to question

---

[278] As read in The US House of Representatives by Congressman Albert S Herlong 1963: http://www.uhuh.com/nwo/communism/comgoals.htm.

time.

Year 9 and 10 History incorporated a series of "empathy tasks" in which we had to emotionally recount the hardships of an Aborigine, an immigrant, and a suffragette. If that wasn't tendentious enough we were then subjected to the cult-like status of Gough Whitlam, the notion that multiculturalism has replaced an Australian national identity, and Australia's "racist" history dating back to the White Australia Policy. HSC Extension History was perhaps even worse as every attempt was made to dispel the notion of "truth" and "facts" in history. Post-modernist homogeneity amongst students seemed to be the aim as it was explained that "the only truth in history is that there is no truth". Left-wing bias in our schools does not originate from the National Curriculum; it is already entrenched and awaiting its full flowering under the National Curriculum.

In 2008 the Young Liberal Movement under the Presidency of Noel McCoy led a *Make Education Fair* campaign which uncovered an avalanche of evidence that our schools and universities have an inherent left-wing bias. The huge success of this grassroots campaign forced the Rudd Government to establish a Senate Inquiry into Academic Freedom. The Young Liberal Movement's 105-page submission to the inquiry highlighted the problems even before there were plans for the National Curriculum.[279] So how does the National Curriculum make things even worse?

The National Curriculum
The first problem with the National Curriculum was the appointment of "former" communist Stuart Macintyre to write the framework for the History component. Whilst this appointment gained little publicity, imagine what the response would have been from left-wing activists and media outlets had John Howard appointed a scholar such as Keith Windschuttle to draft the History curriculum two years earlier.

The second problem lies in the way in which the National Curriculum has been framed. Every subject in it must be taught through three broad themes: indigenous, Asian, and environmental sustainability. How

---

[279] Academic Freedom Senate Inquiry, Submission 43, *Make Education Fair* 2008.

would a teacher even be able to explain to a class why mathematics or science needs an indigenous or Asian context? Why not an Anglo-Saxon or European context? Why is a context, theme or perspective even needed to teach calculus or chemistry? The fact that such perspectives are mandatory in the National Curriculum can only be put down to ideology.

Unsurprisingly the History curriculum is the most unbalanced of the four compulsory subjects, followed by English. English as Australia's official language is undermined in the curriculum by such comments as "English is one of the many languages spoken in Australia" and "Standard English is one of many social dialects used in Australia".[280] Education commentator and academic, Kevin Donnelly, published a brilliant *Quadrant* article 'The Ideology of the National English Curriculum' which argued that "on reading the National English Curriculum, one can envisage the situation where students experience ten years of school without any encounter with such seminal authors as Shakespeare, Swift, Dickens, Austen, Orwell, Lawson or Malouf".[281] Furthermore, even if Shakespeare is taught it must be through an ideological perspective, such as feminism, post-modernism, Marxism, queer theory, and various other 'isms' that John Howard called "gobbledygook".[282]

Whilst Leftist ideology permeates every subject in the National Curriculum, it is important to focus on History, where the bias is starkest. Harmony Day, NAIDOC week, Buddha Day, and National Sorry Day are raised to the same level of importance as ANZAC Day or Christmas Day. Likewise, women's movements and indigenous rights dominate whilst the Magna Carta, the English Bill of Rights and the English Civil War are ignored "rather like an embarrassing relative at Christmas Day lunch", as Christopher Pyne has written.[283]

Conservatism and liberalism as political movements are ignored whilst socialism, nationalism, imperialism and Darwinism are included.

---

280 Kevin Donnelly, 'The Ideology of the National English Curriculum', *Quadrant Magazine*, May 2010.
281 Ibid.
282 Editorial, 'Giving out bad Marx', *The Australian*, 22/04/2006.
283 Dan Harrison and Anna Patty, "Flawed' national curriculum faces axe under Coalition', *Sydney Morning Herald*, 31/01/2011.

Likewise, the cultural geniuses of the Renaissance like DaVinci and Michelangelo are absent whilst AC/DC and Kylie Minogue get a mention. However, even if the content was reweighted slightly more in favour of Western Civilisation, the fact is that "everything must be taught through a PC prism" and "the underlying philosophy is cultural relativism".[284] In other words, changing the content of the National Curriculum is one battle, but changing the way the content is taught in an attempt to reduce teaching bias is an even more difficult task.

So what wasn't I taught in High School History? It can be summed up in two words: Western Civilisation. The National Curriculum has now entrenched this shortcoming federally, with John Howard accurately explaining that:

The Curriculum does not properly reflect the undoubted fact that Australia is part of Western Civilisation; in the process it further marginalises the historic influence of the Judeo-Christian ethic in shaping Australian society and virtually purges British history from any meaningful role.[285]

Of course curricula cannot include everything and choices need to be made. Nevertheless the pendulum has now swung so strongly against Western Civilisation that we are condemning our students to ignorance on the very foundations that underpin Australian society, namely: Christianity, capitalism, the nation-state, law, democracy and freedom.

Christianity

It is impossible to study Western Civilisation without studying Christianity. Western Civilisation was born in Europe and then exported to every corner of the globe. However, Europe is, or at least was for the best part of the last two millennia, a Christian continent. But why is it even important to study Christianity in a 21st Century secular society? Isn't it out-dated, antiquated and the source of more evil than good in the world? Surely we have now 'evolved' to a point where Christianity,

---

[284] Kevin Donnelly, 'History curriculum sacrifices Western values at the altar of political correctness', *The Australian*, 16/03/2013.
[285] John Howard, 'The Importance of Knowing Where We Came From', *Quadrant*, December 2012.

having served its purpose, can now be relegated to the dustbin of history and ultimately forgotten? Such was the view of advocates of the so-called 'secularisation thesis' up until the late 1960s. It seems that just as the world's top scholars have begun asserting the huge importance of religion in history and present-day global affairs, Australian schools are scratching it out of national historical consciousness.[286]

Christianity is the source of much good in the world and to this day underpins the morality of Western nations, even if the Left are unwilling to acknowledge it. Christianity repudiated many of the immoral practices of the ancient world such as polygyny, prostitution, bestiality and infanticide. Women and children were little more than slaves in Roman society, but with Christianity the institution of natural marriage and the building of orphanages helped protect these minorities and lift them to a higher social standing. Praise also has to be given to Christianity for the abolition of slavery, property rights for women, developing charities, creating arguably the first hospitals, education for both sexes, human rights, democracy, capitalism, science, and the best art, architecture, music and literature of all the ages. The achievements of Christianity and how it underpins Western Civilisation and the modern world is very well documented and analysed in Professor Alvin Schmidt's *How Christianity Changed the World*, and more recently in B. S. Gregory's *The Unintended Reformation: How a Religious Revolution Secularized Society*.[287]

Sadly, the Left today want us to ignore, forget and discard the invaluable role that Christianity has had worldwide. The National Curriculum has gone to extreme lengths to expunge references to Christianity. A good example of this is how it removed AD and BC as a dating system, replacing it with the politically correct "common era" [CE] and "before common era" [BCE]. How would a teacher explain to a class when the Common Era begins without reference to Christ? It defies common sense and is just one example amongst many of how the National

---

286 Revisionist scholarship on secularisation is vast. An important recent contribution is C. Calhoun, M. Juergensmeyer, and J. VanAntwerpen (eds.), Rethinking Secularism, Oxford: Oxford University Press, 2011. The writings of Rodney Stark, Phillip Jenkins, and Peter Harrison also illustrate the point that the Whiggish secularist teleology – culminating in the irrelevance of religion in present society – is an ideological retrojection upon the past.

Curriculum has been hijacked by the Left for political purposes.

Most importantly, Australian society has to be based on some sort of morality, what we could call public morality. There is no neutral or unbiased sense of universal morality. One of the best jurists of all time, Lord Denning, best explained the idea of a public morality in his famous quote "Without religion there is no morality, and without morality there is no law".[288] So on what religion do we base Australian morality and law? Should it be Hinduism, Buddhism, or Islam? Or should it be Christianity, the religion that made Australia and Western Civilisation the envy of the world?

In 2002 the Chinese Academy of Social Sciences drew the conclusion that the superiority of Western Civilisation was based upon Christianity rather than advanced military technology or Western economics. They argued that: "In the past 20 years, we have realised that the heart of your culture is your religion: Christianity….The Christian moral foundation of social and cultural life was what made possible the emergence of capitalism and then the transition to democratic politics. We don't have any doubt about this."[289] This simple point may be acknowledged by over 60%[290] of Australians who are Christian and billions of people worldwide. However, the Left ideologues in the Teacher's Federation clearly have not grasped the concept. No religion has given so much to the world and been attacked so viciously as Christianity.

This vicious attack against Christianity usually comes from the proponents of relativism. Many 'academic' Leftists believe that all religions and moral codes are equal, except Christianity, which is evil and should be repudiated. Under the guise of relativism they have attempted to indoctrinate students into believing that truth and morality do not have an absolute foundation, that relativism is the order of the day. Pope Benedict XVI was one of the harshest critics of relativism, especially when it came to education. Shortly after his Papal Inauguration in 2005 Benedict elevated the issue into public debate:

---

288 Lord Denning, *The Changing Law*, London: Stevens and Sons, 1953, p.99.
289 As quoted by Cardinal Pell: http://www.spectator.co.uk/australia/5880128/the-key-to-our-civilisation/
290 2011 Australian Census.

> Today, a particularly insidious obstacle to the task of <u>educating</u> is the massive presence in our society and culture of that relativism which, recognizing nothing as definitive, leaves as the ultimate criterion only the self with its desires. And under the semblance of freedom it becomes a prison for each one, for it separates people from one another, locking each person into his or her own "ego". With such a relativistic horizon, therefore, <u>real education</u> is not possible without the light of the truth....[291]

Pope Benedict XVI could easily have made that exact statement in a newspaper article or a Senate Inquiry into the National Curriculum; no truer words have been spoken. Not all religions are equal because not all religions preach the same morality. If we took a relativist approach to government and law making, Australia would allow genital mutilation, domestic violence and forced marriages simply because a very small minority may view such practices as moral. If we deem that such practices are in fact immoral then doesn't this contradict relativism? Aren't we then basing Australian morality on some sort of moral vantage point, probably a lingering Christian consciousness, and discounting the relativist worldview from which the National Curriculum was written?[292]

Depicting Christianity as the foundation for Western Civilisation in the National Curriculum should be an essential element of our education system; it is far more important than understanding other remote cultures and religions. According to George Weigel, Christianity has done more to promote and defend human rights globally than the United Nations; however, it has suffered unparalleled attacks from the Left.[293] The first step of the Teachers Federation to destroying Christianity in Australia may well be by removing it from the education system. However, they should perhaps heed the words of the great poet T S Eliot: "If Christianity goes, the whole of our culture goes. Then you must start painfully again, and you cannot put on a new culture readymade... You

---

[291] Pope Benedict XVI *Address to the Participants in the Ecclesial Diocesan Convention of Rome* 2005.
[292] On the concept of "smuggling" moral norms in through ostensibly morally neutral or "secular" terms, see Steven D. Smith, *The Disenchantment of Secular Discourse*, Cambridge, MA: Harvard University Press, 2010.
[293] George Weigel *The Cube and the Cathedral*, New York: Basic Books, 2005.

must pass through many centuries of barbarism."[294]

Capitalism

If one looks at any indicator of income, GDP per capita, wealth, economic development, life expectancy, education, or standard of living, the West will generally be ranked at the top. Capitalism, not natural resources nor simply a set of coincidences, was one of the strongest contributors to Western dominance. Hong Kong, Singapore, and to some extent, Japan, are nations with almost no valuable natural resources. They do not have huge deposits of coal, oil or gas, large forests, expansive agricultural land, or iron ore. Singapore and Hong Kong even have to import water from Malaysia and Mainland China just for domestic household use. Although not strictly Western nations, Japan, Hong Kong and Singapore embraced capitalism and their economies rapidly grew up to Western levels. There is no doubt that capitalism is a primary driver of progress and wealth creation.

Governments cannot create wealth; they can only redistribute it. In a capitalist economy 'the consumer is king', as individuals determine the forces of supply and demand (and price) through purchasing goods and services that will increase their utility or self-interest. The father of modern economics, Adam Smith, argued that whilst charity is both honourable and moral it cannot alone deliver what is necessary for living, as "It is not from the benevolence of the butcher, the brewer, or the baker, that we can expect our dinner, but from their regard to their own interest".[295]

The rise of the corporation, increasing trade and output, the Industrial Revolution, division of labour and higher standards of living are all closely related to each other since their inception in the late 18th to early 19th centuries. The corporation developed organically over time since the Roman Republic, however, with the development of limited liability and a perpetual lifetime for corporations in Britain in the early 19th century, the growth (in quantity and size) of corporations exploded.[296] It would

---

294 T. S. Eliot, *Notes Towards the Definition of Culture*, London: Faber and Faber, 1948, p. 200.
295 Adam Smith, *An Inquiry into the Nature and Causes of the Wealth of Nations*, London: W. Strahan and T. Cadell, 1776, Book I, Chapter 2.
296 The Joint Stock Company Act (1844) and the Limited Liability Act (1855) created the

have been impossible to create modern global finance and share markets without this important development in the West. It is arguable whether the Industrial Revolution created the corporation, or if it was the other way around. Certainly the two grew exponentially alongside each other and were necessary for each other's immense success. Nevertheless the Left worldwide has attacked the Industrial Revolution and the corporation despite their immense contribution to our way of life. For example, the 2003 film *The Corporation* written by Marxist professor, Joel Bakan, is a stellar example of the visceral hatred that the Left have for capitalism.[297] Such ideology permeates the education institutions; I remember being forced to watch this "documentary" at the University of Sydney two years ago. To ensure 'balance', the film also included interviews with Noam Chomsky and Michael Moore.

What they failed to teach us was that the Industrial Revolution, capitalism and the growth of corporations created higher standards of living across the board in Western nations. During the Industrial Revolution real average incomes per person immensely improved[298] and child mortality in London declined from 74.5% (1730-1749) to 31.8% (1810-1829). The huge population growth over this time period was not due to an increase in births, but to a decrease in deaths brought about by a more stable food supply and better personal and social hygiene.[299]

Britain became the workshop for the world, and then Europe and America followed. The gap between Western nations and the rest of the world grew largely due to capitalism. However, trade was an invaluable component in the rise of capitalism. Adam Smith and David Ricardo were the two British economists responsible for the theory behind free trade. Adam Smith, in the canonical text the *Wealth of Nations,* was the first to argue that "If a foreign country can supply us with a commodity cheaper than we ourselves can make it, better buy it of them with some

---
modern corporation and modern capitalism.
297 The Corporation (film) written by Joel Bakan, Directed by Mark Achbar and Jennifer Abbott, 2003.
298 Nicholas Crafts and Knick Harley, 'Output Growth and the British Industrial Revolution: A Restatement of the Crafts-Harley View', *Economic History Review*, 45 (1992): pp.703-730.
299 M. C. Buer, *Health, Wealth and Population in the Early Days of the Industrial Revolution*, London: George Routledge and Sons, 1926.

part of the produce of our own industry, employed in a way in which we have some advantage."[300] However, it was David Ricardo who was most responsible for devising the theory of comparative advantage or relative opportunity cost.[301] With entire nations specialising and trading, there came the development of the division of labour; productivity growth meant that more goods and services could be produced in a shorter time.

Capitalism has changed the world for the better, it has led to enormous increases in the standard of living for those living in the West, even if it must endure the many unsubstantiated attacks from socialists whose very policies harm the exact people that they claim they wish to help. Despite this fact, the National Curriculum "is hostile to the role of private enterprise and capitalism,"[302] if it is even taught at all. Capitalism is so irrelevant to the National Curriculum that John Howard rather comically wrote an article in *The Australian* under the title 'Bizarre History curriculum studies Kylie not capitalism'.[303] I certainly was not taught about the benefits of capitalism at my high school and I'm sure that most students would recall a similar experience.

The Nation State

The nation state has developed organically since its inception in Western Europe at the Peace Treaty of Westphalia in 1648. There are essentially two concepts behind the nation state. Firstly, states hold territorial sovereignty and secondly, such territory is based on nationality and the idea of what Edmund Burke would call "a people".[304] The Peace Treaty of Westphalia created the basis of national self-determination and ensured that sovereign states would have a monopoly over the use of (military) force. As the nation state slowly developed in Europe from 1648, the rest of the world was still divided into empires, tribes, city-

---

300 Adam Smith, *An Inquiry into the Nature and Causes of the Wealth of Nations*, London: W. Strahan and T. Cadell, London, 1776, Book IV, Chapter 2.
301 David Riccardo *On the Principles of Political Economy and Taxation*, John Murray, 1817.
302 John Roskam, Executive Director of the Institute of Public Affairs, "What is missing from Australia's National Curriculum, and Why?" *ABC* 7 April 2011.
303 John Howard, 'Bizarre History Curriculum studies Kylie not Capitalism', *The Australian*, 28 September 2012.
304 "A people" is a common theme throughout both Burke's *Reflections on the Revolution in France* and *An Appeal from the New to the Old Whigs*.

states and dynasties all employing private armies and mercenaries with no real concept of nationality or territorial sovereignty.

As the nation state is unique to Western Civilisation why is it important and why should it be taught and celebrated rather than forgotten? Quite possibly the best defence of the nation state can be found in the first chapter of Roger Scruton's 2006 book *A Political Philosophy*.[305] To Scruton, national loyalty is the glue that holds a sovereign state together. In the absence of national loyalty, democracy becomes dangerous and disunited, which could bring about a failed state. 'For without national loyalty opposition is a threat to government, and political disagreements create no common ground', explains Scruton.[306] Nationality binds together all countrymen and women of all classes, faiths, interests, and backgrounds.

Prosperity, democracy, unity, property and peace within a given territory are virtually impossible without the existence of the nation state and the loyalty of the people to it. Edmund Burke knew this even prior to the bloody and tumultuous French Revolution:

> a nation is not an idea only of local extent, and individual momentary aggregation, but it is an idea of continuity, which extends in time as well as in numbers, and in space. And this is a choice not of one day, or one set of people, not a tumultuary giddy choice; it is a deliberate election of ages and generations, it is a Constitution made by what is ten thousand times better than a choice, it is made by the peculiar circumstances, occasions, tempers, dispositions, and moral, civil and social habits of the people, which disclose themselves only in a long space of time. It is a vestment which accommodates itself to the body.[307]

Patriotism is a healthy by-product of national loyalty and the "symbols of national loyalty are neither militant nor ideological, but consist in peaceful images of the homeland, of the place where we belong".[308] Patriotism is not nationalism or fear mongering, but it does ensure that "Our people can quickly unite in the face of threat, since

---

305 Roger Scruton, *A Political Philosophy*, New York: Continuum 2006.
306 Ibid, p.1.
307 Edmund Burke, 'On the Reform of Representation in the House of Commons (1782)', in *The Works of Edmund Burke*, vol.5, Boston: Charles C. Little and James Brown, 1839, p.405.
308 Scruton, *A Political Philosophy*, pp.17-18.

they are uniting, in defence of the thing that is necessary to all of them – their territory".[309] Certainly Churchill's 'we'll fight them on the beaches' speech is a brilliant, albeit clichéd, example of rallying *all* the British people on the grounds of territorial sovereignty and national loyalty.

The Left certainly would never want the virtues of the nation state being taught in schools as part of the National Curriculum. To them the nation state should be broken down and world government should reign supreme. The European Union is the first step in their utopian dreams, even if the majority of ordinary people view it as nothing short of a failed experiment. The Left would prefer to attempt to create a new society and human psyche by experimenting with untried and unconventional means rather than by building on the tried and true foundations that have made Western civilisation the envy of the world. It was Europe's diversity of numerous nation states, rather than a single Empire, that created competition and rivalry. Five hundred years ago an observer might have looked East to the great Empires (Ming, Mogul, Ottoman) and thought that it would be the Chinese who would travel around the world to find Europe rather than the other way around. One reason why it was the Europeans is to be found in the superiority of the nation state over the empire.

On his 2012 Australia tour with the Institute of Public Affairs, Eurosceptic British MEP Daniel Hannan, offered an explanation of why Europe eclipsed Asia:

> Precisely because there was competition, there was a rivalry. You could pilot and trial new ideas and copy what worked elsewhere. You could take your ideas as an entrepreneur round to different governments, as Christopher Columbus did. Or as a government you could send out your agents the way Peter the Great did and say 'look at what works elsewhere, how do the English do their theatre, how do the Dutch do their ships, how do the French do their cannons, let's copy what works best'. Basic conservative free-market principles that apply within a nation also apply among nations.[310]

Sociologist Max Weber acknowledged the importance of competition

---

309 Ibid.
310 Daniel Hannan MEP 2012, http://www.abc.net.au/radionational/programs/counterpoint/the-european-union3a-a-failed-experiment/3850572#transcript.

and rivalry amongst European Nation States: "the competitive struggle (among the European nation states) created the largest opportunities for modern western capitalism."[311] However, today's left-wing academics and union officials at the Teacher's Federation have no such appreciation of the nation state. Western Civilisation and the vital role that Europe and the Nation State has played in our development as Australians is sidelined for the teaching of Polynesia, Rudd's National Sorry Day and, of course, environmental sustainability.

Law

Almost every state worldwide has adopted Western-style legal systems, whether Civil Law or Common Law. The rule of law, separation of powers, the presumption of innocence, the role of evidence, property rights, equality under the law, separation of church and state and religious liberty more broadly are all virtually unique to Western civilisation. Communist nations failed to recognise property rights; many nations (especially those under Sharia Law) failed to uphold religious liberty; and a plethora of tribes failed to achieve both statehood and written law generally. Most importantly, almost every nation and group of people outside of the West failed to uphold the rule of law.

Until such time as the West exported the rule of law across the globe most other nations were subjected to legal systems where the monarch and in some cases aristocrats and religious leaders were above the law. Without the rule of law the elite can ignore their own laws or merely change the law on a whim for their own benefit. Behind Western civilisation there is a long proud historical development of the rule of law, from Aristotle to America in 1776. The rule of law is etched into the social fabric of Great Britain; when threatened by various monarchs it was the rule of law and not monarchical power that triumphed. The nobles of 1215 forced King John to sign the Magna Carta thereby restoring their ancient liberties and the rule of law. Similarly it was the rule of law, rather than the divine right of kings, that was victorious in both the English Civil War (1651) and the Glorious Revolution (1688). Although the Left today may claim bi-partisan support for the rule of law, they rank protestors and

---

311 Max Weber, *General Economic History*, F. Knight (tr.), London: Allen and Unwin, 1923, p.249.

minorities above the law. A good example of this support for minorities was the Greens supporting the Whitehaven Coal Hoax.

Protestors and minorities being given privileges above the law is just one reason why the Left is antipathetic towards the rule of law.[312] The other reason is simply that the rule of law is a Western institution, one that Australia inherited from Britain, and consequently must be imperialist, out-dated and racist and most certainly not worthy of being taught in schools. However, one only needs to look at the Corruption Perceptions Index to see what a positive influence the rule of law has had in Western nations.[313]

How convenient that something as important as the Magna Carta was left out of the draft National Curriculum.[314] John Howard argued that British history is being purged from the National Curriculum for ideological reasons:

> The influence of British institutions on Australia is a fact, not nostalgia: Magna Carta, parliamentary democracy, the language we speak....We cannot know modern Australia well without understanding the British story. How can young Australians ever be expected to understand how fragile and hard-won the rule of law is, without knowing a little about the English Civil War?[315]

Common Law, Civil Law and Roman Law are all Western concepts worthy of being taught in our schools. Professor Wolfgang Kasper strongly argues that it is legal institutions such as Roman Law and property rights that explained "why innovators prospered in the West, and why the West grew rich".[316] There is a stellar historical narrative behind Australia's legal system but unfortunately it is a narrative that our students will never learn.

---

312 Legal double standards, positive discrimination and examples such as Part 18C of the Racial Discrimination Act set to put minorities above the law.
313 Corruption Perceptions Index 2012, Transparency International: http://www.transparency.org/cpi2012/results
314 The Magna Carta was left out of the draft National Curriculum, however it has since been included. Many right-leaning opinion leaders were particularly vocal on this issue.
315 John Howard, 'The Importance of Knowing Where We Came From', *Quadrant*, December 2012.
316 Wolfgang Kasper, *The Merits of Western Civilisation*, Institute of Public Affairs, 2011, p.13.

Democracy & Freedom

A poll conducted by the Lowy Institute in 2012 found that only 39% of those aged 18 to 29 preferred democracy to any other kind of government.[317] Equally alarming, another poll by the Institute of Public Affairs found that only a bare majority (53%) of those aged 18 to 24 believed that the government should not regulate the opinions published in newspapers.[318] In both polls older Australians were strongly more in favour of both democracy and freedom of speech. Younger Australians should be taught the glories of democracy, freedom and Western civilisation like their parents and grandparents were.

Democracy and freedom are part of the fabric of Australian society. In John Howard's *Quadrant* article on the National Curriculum he strongly defends the need for this to be taught:

> There are many components of the Australian achievement. Unlike many other countries we were able to create a functioning democratic political system without ever resorting to violence or conflict.... The fundamental freedoms of Australia are protected by our robust parliamentary system, a highly ethical judiciary and a free and vigorous press, all of which are part of the Western liberal tradition.[319]

When freedom is mentioned in the National Curriculum it is generally part of a broader section on rights, which supposedly stem from the United Nations. The long classical liberal tradition of fighting for the inalienable rights and freedoms of all people is ignored, as is any mention of natural law or freedom emanating from God or the Judeo-Christian ethos. Some on the Left despise democracy and freedom and the others have subverted its teaching and application so as to indoctrinate students into believing that rights, freedoms and even morality stem from United Nations Charters and Declarations. Were we just living in an anarchic moral vacuum prior to the inception of the United Nations?

Almost 200 years before the creation of the United Nations Immanuel Kant argued that freedom is special because it brings out the best in us.[320] A little later Alexis De Tocqueville argued that for democracy to

---

317 Quoted by Institute of Public Affairs: http://ipa.org.au/news/2676/democracy-in-doubt
318 Ibid.
319 Howard 'The Importance of Knowing Where We Came From'.
320 As quoted by Wolfgang Kasper *The Merits of Western Civilisation*, Institute of Public

succeed every citizen must hold indisputable rights and freedoms that cannot be taken away simply with the "tyranny of the majority".[321] When Australia federated in 1901 it was not influenced by the United Nations, which was to form some forty-four years later. Instead our founding fathers were heavily influenced by developments in Western Civilisation, such as the American Declaration of Independence, the English Civil War, the Glorious Revolution, and as such we inherited institutions like Westminster Parliamentary democracy from the United Kingdom and a Federation style model with a Senate from the United States. We cannot cut ourselves off from Western civilisation, as Australians we are its children.

The Leftists who drafted the National Curriculum should have at least attempted to place some emphasis on negative freedom or freedom from the state,[322] rather than just emphasizing the social rights that were supposedly granted to us by the United Nations. After all, "The role of the State is to guarantee order, to ensure that human society does not descend into hell. But the State does not hold the keys to paradise".[323]

The Future

Western Civilisation is underpinned by Christianity, capitalism, the nation state, law, democracy and freedom. These pillars of Western Civilisation were exported around the globe; Australia, as a very young nation, is one of its main beneficiaries. Samuel Huntington in his *Clash of Civilisations* divides the world into many different civilisations, such as: Western, Latin American, Orthodox, Muslim, Chinese, Hindu and so forth.[324] Australia is no doubt a part of Western civilisation along with Western Europe, New Zealand, Canada and the United States of America.

To deny that Australia is part of Western civilisation is to deny our history. Christianity, democracy or the rule of law did not just

---

Affairs, 2011.
321 "Tyranny of the majority" is a common theme in the works of Alexis de Tocqueville, including *Democracy in America* 1835 and 1840.
322 Isaiah Berlin, 'Two Concepts of Liberty', in *Four Essays on Liberty*, Oxford: Oxford University Press, 1969.
323 P. Nemo, *What is the West?*, Pittsburgh: Duquesne University Press, 2007.
324 Samuel Huntington, *The Clash of Civilisations*, New York: Simon & Schuster, 1996.

miraculously one day appear in Australia. They developed over a long period and underpinned European society long before they arrived in Australia. We are at risk of educating an entire generation of students in Aboriginal history, Asian history and environmental sustainability but with no emphasis placed on the Western institutions, values and ideas that form the foundation of Australian society.

Christianity, capitalism, the nation state, law, democracy and freedom are neglected or absent topics at high schools across New South Wales and Australia. It is hard believe that anybody could argue that a feminist-Marxist interpretation of King Lear provides a more valuable education. The content and the tone of education has been biased against Western Civilisation for decades now, however, the National Curriculum has entrenched and centralised this bias.

As conservatives and libertarians, our vision for an Australian education system must include the abolition of the National Curriculum and restoring such power to the States. Even previously supportive figures of a National Curriculum, such as John Howard, now admit that "if something is to be done about this curriculum then only the state governments and, in particular, their education ministers can do it"[325]. Centralising the curriculum in Canberra has just made it easier for the Left to distort it.

Having eight different curricula (one per state and territory) inevitably has its problems, however, it makes it more difficult for the Left to hijack and according to Dr Kevin Donnelly will improve education outcomes through bringing decisions to a more local level, a principle known as subsidiarity.[326] Similarly, we should support Donnelly's vision in so far as:

> Schools should also have the freedom to withdraw from the national curriculum and be given the flexibility to implement acceptable alternatives, either designed locally or chosen from overseas. Schools, such as Montessori, Steiner and faith-based schools, should not be forced into adopting a secular curriculum that, in many instances, contradicts and undermines their educational philosophy.[327]

---

325 John Howard 'The Importance of Knowing Where We Came From'.
326 Kevin Donnelly, 'Schools Forced to Dance to Canberra's Centralist Tune', *The Australian*, 19/12/2012.
327 Kevin Donnelly, 'Flexibility needed in National Curriculum', *The Drum*, 24/11/2011:

Finally, the History curriculum is in desperate need of a radical overhaul, regardless of what level of government is granted responsibility. The history of Western Civilisation must be restored to an important and meaningful part of the curriculum. This in no way means that Australian history or world history has to be forgotten. Greg Melleuish has the correct approach here, advocating for "the need to get the balance right between the study of national history, world history and Western Civilisation".[328] Aboriginal and Asian history can easily co-exist alongside the study of Western institutions, they are in no way mutually exclusive.

Without the abolition of the National Curriculum and a more balanced approach to history education we are condemning our future generations to ignorance. Conservatives and libertarians cannot stand idly by and watch the socialists slowly march through our institutions.

---

http://www.abc.net.au/unleashed/3691354.html.
328 Greg Melleuish, *Is the West Special?*, Institute of Public Affairs, 2012.

www.ingramcontent.com/pod-product-compliance
Ingram Content Group UK Ltd.
Pitfield, Milton Keynes, MK11 3LW, UK
UKHW041414180426
11947UKWH00007B/135